THE REDFISH BOOK

A Complete Angler's Guide

by

Frank Sargeant

Book II in the Inshore Library

A LARSEN'S OUTDOOR PUBLISHING BOOK
THE ROWMAN & LITTLEFIELD PUBLISHING GROUP, INC.
Lanham ▪ Chicago ▪ New York ▪ Toronto ▪ Plymouth, UK

Published by
LARSEN'S OUTDOOR PUBLISHING
An imprint of The Rowman & Littlefield Publishing Group, Inc.
4501 Forbes Boulevard, Suite 200, Lanham, Maryland 20706
http://www.rlpgtrade.com

Estover Road, Plymouth PL6 7PY, United Kingdom

Distributed by National Book Network

British Library Cataloguing in Publication Information Available

Library of Congress Cataloging-in-Publication Data Available

Library of Congress 91-90328

ISBN: 978-0-936512-12-6 (paper : alk. paper)

♾™ The paper used in this publication meets the minimum
requirements of American National Standard for Information
Sciences—Permanence of Paper for Printed Library Materials,
ANSI/NISO Z39.48-1992.

Printed in the United States of America

ACKNOWLEDGEMENTS

I'm indebted to dozens of guides, biologists and expert anglers from throughout the range of the redfish for the contents of this book. Among the guides who were particularly helpful are Doug Bird, master of the Laguna Madre in Texas and Ronny Groinier and Terry Shaughnessy in the bayou country of Louisiana. In Florida, thanks to Oscar Lee at Apalachicola Bay, Frank Schiraldi at Crystal River, Earl Waters and Mike Locklear at Homosassa, Dennis Royston at Hudson, Paul Hawkins, Russ Sirmons, James Wood and Jim O'Neal at Tampa Bay, Scott Moore, Bill Miller and Chris Mitchell at Charlotte Harbor, Kenny Shannon at Venice, Colby Dollar at Homestead and Mike Collins at Islamorada. Ken Lauer, primo surf-caster at the Outer Banks of North Carolina was also a great help, as was Joel Arrington, well-known low-country outdoor writer. Larry Mendez of Shoalwater Boats and Alex Leva of Hydra-Sports were instructive, as was Bob Icenogle of Bob's Machine in Ruskin, Florida, in rigging and running the ultimate redfish boat. And biologist Mike Murphy of Florida's Department of Natural Resources provided all of the research material on the life patterns of redfish. Thanks, too, to all the thousands of Tampa Tribune readers who have shared their secret spots and their know-how with me for all these years, and to the Florida Conservation Association, whose devoted efforts resulted in the current redfish revival in my home state.

COVER: Cover illustration of a battling redfish is by St. Petersburg artist and guide Russ Sirmons. Sirmons sculpts his exquisite works in glass with sandblasting equipment, sometimes taking weeks to perfect a single piece. He accepts commissions to do fish and birds of all species. His telephone number is (813) 526-2090.

PREFACE

This is a book about redfish, or channel bass, or red drum--whatever you call *Sciaenops ocellatus* in your part of the country. Redfish angling is booming throughout the range, from southern Texas to the Outer Banks of the Carolinas, thanks to unprecedented concern among the sportfishing community and widespread passage of tough new laws protecting the species. There are probably more reds and bigger reds in more places today than at any time in the last decade, thanks to control of harvest pressure in nearly every state where the bronze brawlers are found. The redfish recovery, though far from complete, is in full gear throughout the range.

More importantly to the angler, reds are again moving into historic haunts in many parts of their range--the shallow flats where they can be seen before being caught. Sight-fishing adds a whole new dimension to the pursuit of redfish, and has created a whole new generation of enthusiastic redfish anglers. Reds are now recognized as great gamefish, as well as fine table fish. They're one of the great fishery conservation stories of our time.

This book covers where, when and how to find and catch reds in every season of the year, and in each type of habitat where they are found. This information came from literally thousands of hours of "research" with rod in hand, under the tutoring of many of the nation's best redfish anglers--the folks who really wrote this book.

It also touches on the biology, habits and habitat of the species, as well as on their recent history--and on their future--a text being written even now by concerned conservationists, biologists and fishery managers across the country. Hopefully, those who read their words here will come to know and admire this unique species, and become a part of the continuing effort to further the redfish restoration.

(EDITORS NOTE: Limits, seasons and other management rules mentioned throughout THE REDFISH BOOK were current at printing time, but are subject to change by action of state or federal fishery councils. Check local laws before harvesting reds in your area.)

CONTENTS

ABOUT THE AUTHOR

Frank Sargeant is outdoors editor of the Tampa Tribune and a senior writer for Southern Outdoors, Southern Saltwater and BassMaster magazines. He was formerly an editor for CBS Publications Division, and a writer for Disney World Publications, as well as southern editor for Outdoor Life. His writing and photos have appeared in a wide variety of other publications including Field & Stream, Sports Afield, Popular Mechanics, Popular Science and Reader's Digest. He was a fishing guide before becoming a writer and editor. He holds a masters degree in English and Creative Writing from Ohio University, and has taught writing at the high school and college level. He has fished for redfish throughout Florida and the Southeast for more than 20 years. Sargeant lives on the Little Manatee River, near Tampa, Florida.

CHAPTER 1

INTRODUCTION
REDFISH - AN AMERICAN SUCCESS STORY

WATERS LIKE WARM SUMMER BREEZES slide around your bare legs. You wade through fields of waving grass, woman's hair blowing in the tidal wind, where crabs sail like gliding birds, pinfish flirt like butterflies. The surface is slick, molten glass flexing slightly as the last soft swells from distant rage finds the land.

Through this viscous sea comes the sea beast, multi-headed, multi-tailed, in communal motion covering half an acre, a single mind split 500 ways.

Redfish. Coming to your lure.

Time's shutter clicks, the mind framing photographs that will be filed for later viewing in distant places too far removed from the coast.

That moment before the cast when you know the fish are coming to you is the most perfect in angling--all potential, unsullied by the flaws of men and tackle and fish.

You can visualize the perfect angler--you--making the perfect cast to the ultimate fish, the longest, the heaviest, the most heart-strong--and battling him to an heroic end. The line does not fray, the drag does not stick, the rod does not crack in these soft-focused dreams. And both man and fish walk away uninjured by the fray, and better for it.

But red drum don't have time for dreams. They keep moving. If you're not quick about it, they'll be out of range. Coppery torpedoes pushing a metallic hump of water, they are impossible to miss.

But the cast sails out and misses. Short. Amazingly short. (Dammit, you can make that cast 100 times out of 100, why not now?) Now you are playing catch-up, frantically cranking the spoon back to make another try. Lead them, watch the thumb pressure--can't afford a backlash--and let 'er go.

The red drum, Sciaenops ocellatus, is also known as the channel bass, and along the Gulf Coast, as the redfish. The latter name is the term applied to the species throughout this book. Common names also include spot-tail bass, for the ocellated black spot or spots (sometimes up to a half dozen) that appear on the tail, and red bass. Big reds are called "bulls" in most areas, while small ones are called "puppies" or "rats". The back is coppery red, the sides pink to silver, the fins gray blue.

The line is still falling from the sky-arc drawn by the spoon when the strike comes. The white mouth flares and you feel the solid, arm-jolting thump of the heavy body, the wild heart turning for the first time against restraint.

Why does it seem to matter so much if the line breaks? You'll release him anyway. Does it matter if he spools the reel, if the hook pulls?

It shouldn't, but your pulse tells you that it does matter as you flounder along the boiling path of the fish, puffs of mud going up where his landing gear has touched bottom in a wild, ricocheting flight toward freedom. Gain line back, lose it again--don't tighten the drag, you ass! Arms and wrists start to throb with oddly pleasant pain--redfish masochism?

This goes on for about as long as it takes to run a mile, and seems to require about as much energy, until at last the fish lies gasping at your feet.

Pick him up: sea-hardened, the body seems as heavy as metal, and the bronzed back completes the illusion--this is a fish cast in a tropic furnace and still warm from it, not spawned in the sea.

Twist out the hook, grasp the body just in front of the big blue tail, about where the tattoo of the species marks the skin, and bring back the failing life with slow pumps through the water. The fish floats sideways on the first release, still not believing in mercy. The second time, after a few more strokes, it does believe, and swims off in slightly ruffled grace.

For once, the reality has been better than the vision.

That was at Florida's St. Martin's Keys, not long ago.

12

Big reds, shallow water and sundown. It's the making of an angler's dream, available along much of the southern Atlantic and Gulf coasts these days.

The Redfish Revival

But it's the sort of shallow-water fantasy trip that's taking place all along the southeast coast and throughout the Gulf of Mexico these days, because there are more big reds on the coastal flats at present than at any time in the last 20 years.

Thanks to tight restrictions on harvest throughout most of the range of the redfish, there's now a strong crop of fish ranging from 5 to 15 pounds roaming inshore, and the majority of them are being found in water just knee-deep. It's not quite like the good old days--not yet--but it's a far cry from just 10 years ago when a single red of that size often made the local newspapers. It's an angling earthquake on the scale of the Great Lakes salmon debut in the 1970's, the sort of fishing that brings tears to the eyes of old- timers who thought such sights were gone for good with the rise of the beachfront condominiums. And it's currently creating aftershocks in the sale of flats boats, push poles and flyrods, gear designed to take advantage of this "new" flats species found in waters well north of the bonefish flats of the Florida Keys.

A trip I made not long ago with St. Petersburg guide Paul Hawkins is a case in point. Within minutes after leaving the ramp at the Sunshine Skyway Bridge, in the heart of the Tampa/St. Pete metro-plex, Hawkins shut down his outboard and began to pole his shallow-draft bonefish skiff.

"They'll be here," he told me. "They're always here."

He was right. In a sun-silvered cove near a mangrove island, the water began to hump into a traveling "V" the minute we poled into range. It's hard to say how many fish were in that school, but when we closed in on them the whole surface of the lagoon turned bronze-red as the fish all rose near the top at once.

Bigtime mental snapshot. Every one of them was 10 pounds or better.

It was simply a matter of making a short pitch to the front of the pack-- the resulting melee around the gold spoon reminded me of dropping food pellets into a trout hatchery. Paul made a toss with a streamer fly, and also had instant redfish.

On the flats, reds are particularly sporty dream-weavers, because they devote their considerable energies to straightaway runs rather than sulking deep. These did their stuff until both of us were sweating heavily in the July morning. We finally retired them, shot a few photos, and slipped them back to join the school. Ten seconds later, both of us were fast to new fish--and so it went all that morning. The mental camera ran out of film before noon.

The fishing is not restricted to the Tampa Bay area, by any means. It's just as good in nearly every bay and estuarine area from the southern tip of Florida to Brownsville, Texas around the Gulf, and similar action can be found in bays and coastal rivers all the way up the Atlantic shoreline to Chesapeake Bay.

14

Tight regulations now require that most reds be released to complete their life-cycle and add new juveniles to the stocks. The management efforts appear to be paying off throughout the range, though biologists caution that full recovery is probably still a decade away.

Redfish History

It's a far cry from four years ago, when wide-open commercial netting and sportfishing without bag limits had flattened redfish stocks in most parts of the range. Biologists with the Florida Department of Natural Resources estimated that less than 1 percent of juvenile redfish--which grow up in inshore waters--were surviving long enough to reach maturity at 10-12 pounds and migrate offshore to spawn. Depending on whose figures you chose to believe, sportfishermen were taking either 50 percent or 80 percent of that ca   , commercials the rest. (We have found the enemy and he is us--and them.) Many other states were facing up to similar problems--too many fishermen, too few fish.

Further, the "blackened redfish" craze that hit the nation about that time created a huge demand for the adult fish--a demand promptly filled by giant purse seine boats that netted millions of pounds of spawners in the Gulf of Mexico. Though mature reds over 20 pounds are scarcely edible by normal cooking methods, the mix of hot Cajun spices, butter and a smoking hot skillet made them an item in swank restaurants across the nation.

It also endangered the future of the species.

It wasn't long before the stocks hit bottom, but it also wasn't long before the public, at the encouraging of state biologists and conservation groups, woke up to the problem. Broad public support for restrictions combined with biological data to convince both state and federal fishery managers that tight harvest regulations were needed.

The commissions responded with increased size limits and closed seasons for the sportfishermen, a total shutdown of the offshore purse seining, and severe limitations or complete closure on inshore commercial netting, with most of the rules in place by the end of the Eighties.

The results were prompt and remarkable: redfishing of the sort that hasn't been seen in decades in many areas. Biologists say that it will take at least another 10 years before the stocks recover to really healthy levels in all age ranges, but in the meantime, there are great numbers of three- to four-year old reds in thousands of square miles of flats where they were rare before wise management was put into place.

It's a great time to make redfishing dreams come true.

CHAPTER 2

REDFISH COUNTRY

THE RANGE OF THE REDFISH extends throughout the coastline of the southeastern United States. Maryland is the last stronghold northward, though stragglers are occasionally caught all the way to Massachusetts. They're found throughout the curve of the Gulf of Mexico, at least as far south as Vera Cruz, Mexico. Thus, at least 10 states and two nations along some 3,000 miles of shoreline support fishable populations of this drum species.

Gulf Coast Reds

As you'd expect, any fish found over such a broad range is highly adaptable to the available habitat. In the Laguna Madre of Texas, reds are found in clear, knee-deep grass flats. Up the prairie at Galveston, they're caught along the beaches and in the deep, murky ship channels. Jump over to Louisiana bayou country and every muddy creek and blackwater bayou holds juvenile reds in winter. The mouth of the Mississippi River, with a constant 7-knot current of the muddiest water on the continent, is alive with big reds, and the inshore oil rigs are stacked up with fish in the 10-pound class. Run offshore 20 miles or so between Texas and the Florida panhandle and, if you're lucky, you'll encounter a school of jumbo redfish, doing whatever adult reds do for the last 30 years of their lives.

These schools, the mature, 50-pound spawners gathered in masses that allowed purse seiners to take 50,000-pound strikes, are the mother lode of Gulf redfish, the spring from which the rivers of reds flow out to the estuaries around the Gulf. These giants are off-limits to harvest from federal waters under current laws, but they're out there to restore the inshore populations with their spawn, and to provide remarkable catch-and-release action for sportsmen who locate the schools.

Redfish country is commonly an archipelago of mangrove islands, surrounded by shallow grass flats dotted with oyster bars and cut by narrow creeks.

The bays and estuaries along the Alabama coast and the Florida panhandle down to Cedar Key are vast blackwater rearing areas for hundreds of tons of juvenile reds each year.

Florida Redfish

And as you move into the clearer shallower water from Crystal River south, the land of sight fishing for "tailers" opens up around thousands of oyster bars and mangrove islands. This wonderland extends southward to Naples, where the murky waters flowing out of the Everglades puts an end

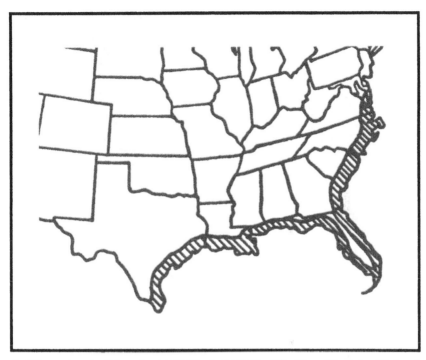

Redfish country extends from the coast of Maryland to the tip of Florida, and throughout the length of the Gulf Coast states. Reds are found at least as far southward as Vera Cruz, Mexico.

to the sight fishing, but not to the redfish--they're thick in the endless, winding creeks and hidden pools of the glades. And there's also good sight fishing here, if you move outside the mangroves to the shallow flats spreading out across Florida Bay toward the Keys.

Not many reds are found in the Florida Keys south of Islamorada, and Biscayne Bay is better known for bonefish than reds. But move northward to where the high-rise buildings become more scarce and the shallow flats begin again--at St. Lucie Inlet--and you again find reds prowling the inshore waters. The Indian River has plenty, as does the Banana River at Cape Canaveral (the ship turning basin is a winter spot for jumbos), Mosquito Lagoon north of the Cape, and the Intracoastal Waterway north to Jacksonville. The lower St. Johns is a noted redfish mine in fall and winter, with thousands of fish in the 5 to 10 pound class gathering in deep, rocky holes. There are plenty of reds northward to Fernandina Beach in the ICW and adjacent rivers, as well.

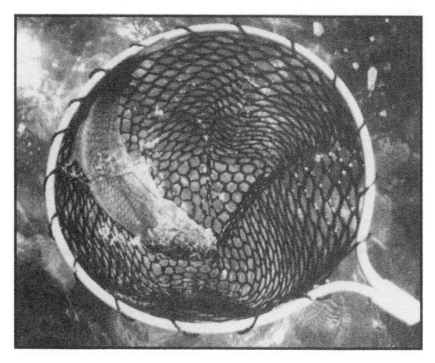

Reds are adaptable fish. They thrive in clear, shallow grass flats, but also do well in the thick mud of the lower Mississippi Delta, in the murky backwaters of the Everglades, and in the coffee-black outflows of rivers along the Atlantic shore. Mature fish spend much of their lives well offshore in the Gulf and Atlantic.

The Atlantic Coast

Beyond the Florida line the blackwater creeks begin to take on a muddy stain with the farm-country rivers flowing out of Georgia, but the reds don't mind the mud. They're caught in the rivers in huge numbers throughout the winter months, and fall brings some "bull" reds to the surf of the coastal islands and passes.

The water turns black again coming out of the Carolina lowland swamps and flowing into the clam country of big bays like Pamlico Sound, the back side of the Outer Banks. The Sound has loads of juveniles, as well as occasional "red waves" of adults in fall, while the true giants of all redfish cruise along the outside beaches. Nearly all the current line class records for channel bass have been set in the fall in this area, and the average size is far superior to that found anywhere else in the redfish range, with 50-pound fish always a possibility.

The current all-tackle record, a stunning 94 pounds, 2 ounces, was taken at Avon, North Carolina, just north of Cape Hatteras, in November of 1984. The second biggest on record, 90 pounds even, was caught at Rodanthe, just 20 miles north of Avon, in November of 1973. And the third largest, 72 pounds, 7 ounces, was also taken in the Hatteras area, also in November of 1973.

In fact, 11 of the current 16 line-class records came from the Outer Banks of North Carolina, and two more came from the adjacent waters of Virginia. Nine of the 10 record N.C. fish were caught in November--get the hint?

There are sometimes good numbers of reds in Chesapeake Bay, in the same country preferred by the much more popular striped bass there. And surf fishermen along the coast of Virginia, Maryland and even New Jersey tangle with stray "bull" reds on occasion.

Thus, redfish country can be darn near anywhere, from the salty water of the open sea to the completely fresh water of a coastal river, 20 miles from the nearest bay. It can be glass-clear or muddy enough to plow. It can be 50 miles at sea or smack against the beach.

That's the great thing about the redfish. Where ever you want to fish, if you learn his habitat preferences and migrations, you're never far from action.

CHAPTER 3

TACKLE FOR REDFISH

REDFISH TACKLE CAN BE ANYTHING from a five-weight flyrod with 2-pound tippet right on up to a 13-foot "Hatteras Heaver" surf rod armed with 300 yards of 30-pound test. The tackle for reds varies so much because the fish vary so much both in size and in the terrain where they're found. Take a gander at David Deuel's all-tackle 94-pound, 2-ounce world record, standing as big as a man, and you'll be convinced that nothing short of marlin gear would do the job on such a beast--and, in fact, the North Carolina lunker was taken on 50-pound tackle.

But for the average red, 5 to 15 pounds, caught in shallow inshore waters, there's no need to overgun yourself. Big tackle makes you tired, spoils the pleasure of landing even a spirited fish, and is tough to use with accuracy.

Reds don't have the disturbing tendencies of snook to go climb a mangrove tree when hooked, either, so you don't need the power to turn them on a short rope. This is one of the blessings of inshore reds, in that they allow the use of tackle that's very light to subdue very substantial fish. When reds are found on the flats with no ready access to deep water, many guides use nothing heavier than 8-pound-test on spinning gear that's basically freshwater bass tackle.

Inshore Spinning Gear

In spinning gear, the determinant is more the bait or lure to be used rather than the ability to control the fish. A long, soft-tipped spinning rod is the ticket for live bait anglers who want to wing a live shrimp or sardine 150 feet, and some guides have special rods made up for the task, using 8-foot flyrod blanks to give them maximum distance. (The West Coast steelhead rod is ideal for this duty, incidentally--long, flexible and able to toss a sardine a mile. Berkley makes a good one, among others.)

When medium-sized reds like this 7-pounder are found in shallow water, light spinning tackle of the sort used for freshwater bass fishing is adequate to subdue them, so long as the reel has a smooth drag and the angler knows how to use it.

The average inshore angler who wants to use his spinning gear for both live bait and artificials up to a half-ounce will be happier, though, with a fairly stiff, 7-foot graphite rod with a two-hand grip and a reel capable of holding around 180-yards of 8-pound-test and weighing 8 to 10 ounces. This is a small, light reel--but you don't need anything bigger to catch inshore redfish, and bigger reels make casting a chore instead of a pleasure. You don't need all that line for the typical inshore fish, of course, but we list capacity to give you an idea of the spool size that works best for rapid retrieves.

One way of determining adequate spine in the rod is to mount a reel of this weight and lean the rod against the wall at about 60 degrees. Those with adequate backbone flex very little in this position, and any bending will be in the last foot at the tip.

The narrow-spool "long-cast" reels definitely do add casting distance with any line test or lure weight, and should be the choice of saltwater anglers these days. Shimano, Daiwa and Garcia, among others, have long-cast models that work well. Fast retrieves are also helpful, with 5:1 gearing the minimum for coastal use.

Inshore Baitcasters

In inshore baitcasters, two-hand, medium/heavy graphite rods designed for lures in the 1/4 to 1 ounce range and measuring 6 to 7 feet are the ticket. The extra length adds extra distance. The flex on these rods should

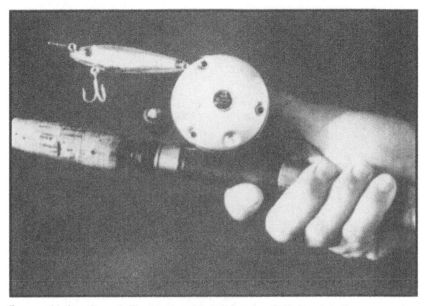

Free-spool baitcasting reels like the venerable Ambassadeur 5000-C and similars, mounted on a two-hand graphite popping rod about 6 1/2 feet long, make an ideal rig for tossing plugs or spoons. Most anglers prefer mono testing 12 to 15 pounds for inshore reds

be minimal, an inch or so when leaned against the wall, reel mounted. The "store feel" is very stiff, like a curtain rod, showing very little whip without a lure attached. The long grip helps ease casting chores and also assists in fighting big fish. Berkley makes some of the premier rods in this class in their Series One, with the B50-7M ideal for reds, snook and even medium-sized tarpon. Daiwa builds similar ones, as does Bass Pro Shops, Cabelas, Orvis, Fenwick and others.

Free-spooling level-wind baitcasters with about 150 yards of 12 pound test mono are right for inshore reds. Again, use a light reel, under 10 ounces, with a smooth drag and stout gears. The Ambassadeur 5000 and 5000C offer longevity and low maintenance, as do Daiwa's ProCaster and Shimano Bantam Speedmasters.

Tackle For Bull Reds

Once the redfish matures and moves offshore to spawn, it might as well be a different species from the inshore juveniles. These brawny giants, scaling 30 to 50 pounds on the average, are far too much fish for flats tackle,

For surf-casting, long rods and big reels are called for to reach out beyond the breakers. Most beginning surf fishermen find it easier to handle spinning gear than revolving-spool reels, though the latter will handle heavier line.

especially in the heavy waves and currents along the ocean surf where they're most often encountered. Add to their bulk and running ability the fact that baits often have to be presented at distances of over 200 feet, and it becomes clear that inshore tackle just won't do the job.

Spinning gear is the favored choice for beginning surf anglers because it doesn't offer the specter of monumental backlashes possible with revolving spool reels. Rods 10 to 12 feet long, designed for lines testing 10 to 30 pounds and lures in the 1- to 6-ounce range are about right. The reels to match should hold at least 200 yards of 20-pound test. These reels are not light, with most scaling close to a pound and a half. Don't worry about high gear ratios with reels this large--the big spool takes care of retrieve speed, and most pros want gearing no higher than 4.5 to 1 to give added power when it's needed. Penn and Daiwa make some good ones.

In revolving-spool gear, rods 8 to 10 feet long and designed to handle lures in the 2- to 6-ounce class are good. The Ambassadeur 7000 or 7000C,

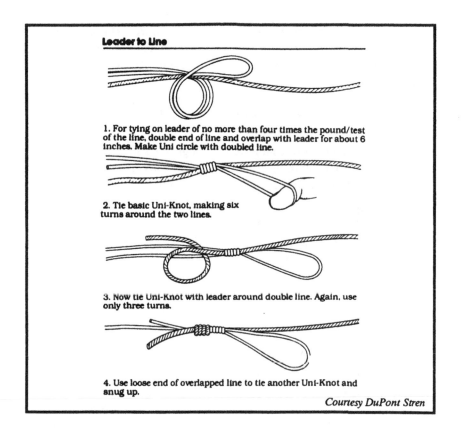

Leader to Line

1. For tying on leader of no more than four times the pound/test of the line, double end of line and overlap with leader for about 6 inches. Make Uni circle with doubled line.

2. Tie basic Uni-Knot, making six turns around the two lines.

3. Now tie the Uni-Knot with leader around double line. Again, use only three turns.

4. Use loose end of overlapped line to tie another Uni-Knot and snug up.

Courtesy DuPont Stren

which holds about 200 yards of 30 pound mono, is a good choice for ease of casting and level wind retrieve, though it might be considered short on capacity around Hatteras, where world-record fish are a possibility at any time. The reel weighs about 20 ounces. Daiwa's Sealine is also good, and Penn makes a wide selection of venerable surf reels that have been around for decades.

Lines

Any quality monofilament will do the job. Redfish are not particularly line shy, so choose any color that pleases your eye. Stren, Trilene, Ande and Silver Thread are among the best. In fishing the surf, you might want to go to some of the abrasion-resistant lines like Trilene XT or DuPont High Impact. These are not usually best for light spinning gear, however; their extra toughness tends to make them a bit wiry and more inclined to jump off the spool and create snarls. For spinning with small, light reels you might choose some of the ultra-thin lines such as Trilene XL or DuPont Magna Thin.

The co-polymer lines I've tried have not been particularly better than quality mono, and considering the extra cost, seem hard to justify in saltwater where changing line after every second day of fishing is standard practice. (In lighter tests, some pros change after a single big fish. They say once the line is stretched to the max, its breaking test is greatly reduced. So buy your line in big spools and be prepared to change often.)

Leaders

Leaders are not essential to catching reds, but if you fish line lighter than 12 pound test add 18 inches of shock leader between running line and lure. This prevents the rough mouth of the redfish from abrading through and acts as a shock absorber when you cast. Without the shock leader, the first foot of line gets a lot of wear from the tip guide and will soon fatigue. The leader also strengthens a loop-knot tied directly to a spoon or other lure with no swivel.

Tie in the shock leader to your running line with a blood knot, Albright special or double Uni-Knot, rather than a swivel. The line-to-line connection goes through the guides easily, does not collect weeds, and is not attractive to line-snipping mackerel and blues. (The exception is when you fish a spoon--then, a small barrel swivel is necessary to keep twist out of your line, as we'll see in the chapter on spoon fishing.)

CHAPTER 4

THE FLORIDA FLATS

FOR FLORIDA REDFISH ANGLERS, the good old days are now. Thanks to several years of completely closed seasons in the late 1980's, followed up by extremely strict harvest regulations that extend to the present, the shallows of the state are now boiling with the greatest crop of sizable reds seen in decades, and inshore anglers by the hundreds are learning how to enjoy the bonanza. Biologists warn that the recovery is not yet complete, but compared to the minimal action of just a few years back, redfishing these days looks great in Florida.

Anglers on the west coast, where clear, shallow grass flats extend through most of the major bays and along the Intercoastal Waterway, are reporting schools of hundreds of fish in the four- to 10-pound range. The action extends all the way from the Panhandle into the Everglades, and has created a "redfish rush" as word spreads of how and where to catch the bull-shouldered brawlers. Fish are similarly abundant on the Atlantic shore, with great fishing reported from the flats of the Intracoastal Waterway, Mosquito Lagoon, the Banana River, and the Indian River. Fish of 20 and even 30 pounds are not uncommon on the east coast flats, and some anglers believe the giants remain there year around, even spawning in the high-salinity waters rather than journeying offshore as they do in more brackish estuaries.

It's a far cry from the scene just five years ago, when most anglers found it tough to locate a single redfish any larger than the foot-long "rats" caught in canals and holes during winter.

In fact, according to biologists, this fishing was a part of the problem. Meat anglers and inshore commercial netters were catching all but .2 percent of the reds before they reached adulthood--few were surviving long enough to reach a size of interest to sport fishermen, fewer still lasting long enough to migrate offshore as adult spawners. Redfish don't spawn until they

This 20-pounder from the Banana River, on Florida's Atlantic Coast, is fully mature and ready to spawn. She was released after the photo.

reach weights of about 10 pounds, which requires dodging the hooks and nets for three to four years in the estuaries.

Further, for a short but devastating period when blackened redfish became a restaurant rage, huge commercial purse seine boats began to target the offshore schools of adults, scooping out 50,000-pound bites from the spawning stock that had always replenished the inshore juvenile population for all Gulf states. Widespread protest by conservationists finally brought a halt to the slaughter via National Marine Fisheries Service rules, but not until millions of pounds of adult reds wound up buried in Cajun spices.

Florida's MFC, with encouragement from the Florida Conservation Association, moved to cut the kill. They finally chose to shut down all harvest when blocked by the Governor and Cabinet, which must approve their rules, from making the species a gamefish. No netting, no sale--and no harvest by recreational anglers. The restrictions were eased in 1988 to allow one fish daily, 18 to 27 inches long, but the shutdown on commercial harvest was wisely kept in place. That rule was made permanent in 1991.

Though many thought the rules too tight when they first went into place,

Reds readily take flies, and are often found in clear, shallow water where sight-fishing is possible.

sport fishermen throughout the state are enjoying the result today in catches that sometimes reach 30 or more fish daily, with many in excess of 10 pounds.

And the most exciting thing about the new abundance is that the fish are being found in shallow water, where sight fishing with light tackle--including fly rods--is possible.

"This is like somebody just invented a new fish," one angler told me. "It's like bonefishing, but when do you ever catch this many 10-pound bones?"

A visit I made to St. Martin's Keys, off the fishing village of Homosassa, is typical of the action many anglers are experiencing these days. Guide Mike Locklear had eased his skiff through perhaps a quarter-mile of knee deep water, so clear that you could have read a newspaper on the bottom, into a slightly deeper pocket between two mangrove islands.

"I'm not sure they'll be here, but a lot of times they are," he whispered as we rigged up gold Johnson Silver Minnow spoons. (I don't know why fishermen whisper when they sneak up on fish, but most of us do.)

The fish were there. My first cast drew a heavy strike, and when the bronzed beauty came steaming by the boat a few seconds later, he had five buddies with him. Every one of them was 8 pounds or better. Mike simply flipped his spoon at them and was instantly hooked up.

Guide Mike Locklear hoists a typical Homosassa red of about 6 pounds. Locklear, formerly a commercial fisherman, is typical of the new breed of conservation-minded guides now battling to improve redfish numbers.

A redfish in shallow water is a far different creature from the same fish in a 30 foot deep hole. As soon as they realize they are in danger--which sometimes takes a minute or so--they depart. If you fish reasonably light line--8 to 10 pound test is adequate--they make your reel play a happy, high-pitched tune. And with reds, the second run--and the third--are likely to be nearly as long as the first.

Locklear staked the boat so that it wouldn't drift down on the fish, and for the next 90 minutes, we caught a red of 8 pounds or better on every cast we threw. When the remaining fish finally spooked, I was glad to see them go--I couldn't have lifted the rod for another one.

Other trips in recent months brought similar results--at Crystal River, at Tampa Bay, at Charlotte Harbor and in the Ten Thousand Islands--some 250 miles of shoreline as the crow flies, probably four times that counting all the redfish bays and creeks and bayous. The redfish wave is widespread, and the fish stay in the shallows almost year around. The only slack period, guides say, is when an extreme front drops temperatures below freezing in January and February. But even then, a few warm days will bring them back.

The shallow water techniques for catching the fish have been pioneered by a few guides like Homosassa's Earl Waters, familiar with flats fishing in the keys. They brought their bonefish skiffs, push poles, and super silent approaches to the more northerly flats, and converted hundreds of anglers in the last few years. In waters where it was a rarity to ever see a flats skiff, there are now dozens of them.

The methods require some practice, however. Learning to handle a shallow draft boat, capable of running in a foot of water and floating in 8 inches or less, is a big part of it. The fish live in areas that simply can't be reached by most larger, deep-vee boats. Smaller boats with semi-vee or flat bottoms, most weighing no more than 800 pounds, are the choice of flats experts.

Reds in the shallows are nearly as spooky as bonefish and permit at times, so it's essential to learn the use of a pushpole for a silent approach--especially when fish are found in water under 18 inches deep. Electric trolling motors are also a great help, though the whirr of the motor sometimes spooks fish in extreme shallows.

The fish are most often found in areas with clear water and lots of sea grass. Rocky island areas such as those off Crystal River and Homosassa are also good, as are locations with plenty of oyster bars--such as the smaller bays on the north side of Charlotte Harbor, or similar locations in the Indian River on the state's east coast.

The angler new to shallow water fishing will be safest to explore on rising water--that way, if you run aground, the tide will soon float you off. In many areas, reds are most active and easiest to find on the rise, too.

Until you begin to know from experience where reds hang out--a school may stay in a range no larger than a football field for months--the only thing to do is to pole the shallows--water one to four feet deep--and keep your eyes

Shallow-draft bay boats make the best redfishing machines for inshore waters. Many expert anglers use their boat to get to a likely flat, then slip overboard to approach the fish at close range.

open for them. Pay particular attention to outside points where tides sweep past an island or oyster bar, and to grass-bottomed bays where the tide flows through, bringing plenty of bait with it.

You need polarized glasses and a cap to shade your eyes so that you can see through the surface glare, and the higher up you can get, the more fish you'll see. That's why many flats boats have a poling platform over the motor. A large ice chest, tied down on the bow, can serve the same purpose for casting.

Sometimes the fish make it easy. Where there are large schools, the fish often create a sizable vee wake as they swim, pushing a hump of water in front of them. It's larger than the wake created by mullet, easily seen hundreds of yards off on a calm day. (And sometimes you can make them show, by putting your boat in a bog, just off plane, as you motor the edge of a flat. The wake and the noise often causes a lazing school to start moving, creating a redfish vee that you can see at several hundred yards. You then shut down the motor and pole to cut them off.)

Redfish also "tail" like bonefish in extremely shallow water. As they tip up to grab a crab on bottom, their bluish tail protrudes through the surface. It's a small target to look for, but with experience it's not hard to see.

And when the sun gets high, you can actually sometimes see a "red wave" as a school rises to move from one spot to another--the water literally turns copper from the light reflecting off the fish's backs.

One of the great things about Florida reds is that they are territorial, and don't like to leave a location once they settle into it. If you spook them off a particular rock point or a slough in the grass, chances are good that if you come back to that spot in an hour, the fish will have returned. And they'll very likely be in the same spot on the same tide tomorrow.

For this reason, some fishermen exploring new areas simply run the flats rapidly on outboard power, looking for fish to boil out in front of them. They note the locations, then return to fish the spots later. (A conservation caution here--don't run your outboard over grass in water where the prop makes contact with the bottom. The "prop trails" created by this are far too abundant, now that inshore fishing has become so popular, and it takes years for the grass to grow back once uprooted.)

Though most anglers fish for reds primarily on the rising tide, fishing can also be excellent on low water. The fish usually don't move more than 300 yards from their high-tide feeding areas when the water falls. Most flats have slightly deeper pockets somewhere along their length, and the fish drop into these. But they do become extremely nervous in the shallower water.

The keys to successfully finding reds on the flats are persistence and mobility. Keep moving and searching likely areas until you actually see fish before you ever pick up a rod. It may make for some long and frustrating hours until you figure out local patterns, but once you have several hotspots located you can return to them repeatedly and find excellent action.

CHAPTER 5

WIGGLE, FLASH AND SQUIRM

IT'S NOT REALLY FAIR to fish live baits for redfish. They're generally so willing to attack artificials that putting the real thing on is overkill.

Except when it's not. Sometimes reds can disappear from all the spots where you absolutely know they ought to be, and the only thing that will make them materialize again is a darting, flashing sardine, a juicy crab or a flipping, high-jumping shrimp. (If you think shrimp don't jump, you haven't seen one with a redfish on his tail.)

Shrimp--Little Bait For Big Fish

Reds of all sizes love shrimp, but young fish like them best. They're the preferred food item for juvenile reds in most areas, and the biggest bull in the surf can't turn down a jumbo.

An awful lot of reds are caught with shrimp anchored to bottom by several ounces of lead, but that's going about it the hard way. It's much more effective to fish them unweighted and let the shrimp fish for you. A shrimp in a spring-loaded harness (Pico and others make them) or hooked lightly under the horn will stay alive for some time, and swim actively enough to turn on any red in the vicinity.

A mistake sometimes made with live shrimp is fishing them on hooks that are too heavy. Heavy wire makes a large hole in the shell, which soon results in a dead shrimp. Even while living, the shrimp can't carry the extra weight very well. It makes sense to fish shrimp unweighted on fine wire hooks--size 1 or 1/0, max, and light spinning gear to get the most from them.

The hook-up under the horn on the head is the most common. Turn the hook sideways and slide the barb in just under the horny crest, avoiding the dark spot below that marks the vitals. The shrimp will swim naturally for extended periods.

Live baits free-lined on light spinning gear are irresistible to redfish. At times when they're hard to locate with artificials, the added action and scent of the real thing can make them materialize.

But if you have to make a long throw to reach the fish, hooking through the last joint of the tail is a better bet since it's a stronger connection. It's also not a bad idea to break off the flipper from the tail on this hook-up, so that the bait doesn't spin in the current. Removing the tail also puts scent into the water, allowing reds to home in on bait they can't actually see.

Shrimp harnesses, mentioned above, also do a good job of keeping shrimp on the hook and lively.

If you fish shallow water, consider the use of a popping cork. These cup-faced foam floats create a chugging sound when they're jerked through the water. Reds home in on the noise, then see or smell the shrimp and you're in business. The float also adds weight to improve casting distance.

Crabs Put The Bite On Reds

Reds eat pretty much anything that happens to get in their way, but they show a preference for certain food items. Take a look down a redfish throat and you'll see the "crushers" that are characteristic of crab eaters, bony pads designed to grind up the shell so that the goodies inside can be put to use in the stomach. So crabs are definitely high on the list of redfish baits.

Inshore fish eat a lot of emergent crabs, those that spend part of their time in water, part on land, such as fiddlers. Fiddlers are easy to find along estuarine shores anywhere a sandpit provides a place to dig their dime-sized holes, and at low water it's no problem to catch several dozen by hand in an area where they're concentrated. Fiddlers sometimes stack up in incredible numbers in secluded tidal creeks, and if you find one of these locations you can depend on plenty of bait for weeks. Fiddlers are not difficult to handle, either, since their single pincher is designed mostly for mating display.

The small, round-bodied black crabs found on oyster bars, seawalls and rip-rap throughout the southeastern coast are also high on the redfish list, but they're quick and usually found only inches from cover, so not an easy bait to collect. Reds eat a lot of them where they're present, though, so you can sometimes use their presence as a mark of a likely shore to fish on high water.

Blue crabs are used as bait more than any other species, primarily because they're very abundant and come in a range of sizes adequate to interest redfish of all ages. They're also easily collected in a box trap baited with fish heads. Small silver-dollar-sized crabs can often be dipped up in the Atlantic or Gulf surf after dark or at dawn, and in spring and summer crabs of this size frequently come drifting through the passes at the surface on strong outgoing tides--much to the delight of redfish in the southern part of the range.

The best blue crabs for most redfishing are about two to three inches across the shell. For the big channel bass of the Carolina surf, adult crabs four to five inches wide are more interesting, and many anglers like to use jumbos, cut in half, to spread the scent.

Blue crabs are easy to keep alive in a bucket of wet moss, they last for hours on the hook, and if you don't catch anything you can always eat the bait. But they do take some special handling.

Blues, in particular, are vicious little characters very capable of scissoring off a hunk of your finger as readily as they dice up a mullet. The wise way to handle them is to remove the claws. Break off the entire arm at the shell

Shrimp are easy to obtain, easy to keep alive, and are deadly for reds of all sizes. They're best fished unweighted, either free-lined or under a popping cork.

and the crab will be much easier to deal with, but will survive for as long as you'll need him.

Crabs are generally fished on short shank, extra-strong hooks. The short shank prevents the hook from interfering with the natural movement of the crab, and the extra-strong wire is needed to force the barb through the hard shell. Put it through one of the points on the blue, or through the back section of a fiddler, to cause minimal injury. Once the point is through, always take a look at it to make sure it has not been dulled by the shell--if so, touch it up with a couple of strokes from a file.

Sardines-Worth Their Weight In Silver

"Sardines" are among the most devastating of all redfish baits. There are a number of flat, silvery baitfish that go by this name, including the scaled sardine, Spanish sardine and the threadfin herring, all very similar, all good baits--though the scaled sardine is probably the most durable in the baitwell. This species, also known as "whitebait", comes readily to chum, which some of the others do not, so it's the most common redfish bait in much of the southeast.

This red homed in on the noise generated by the cork as it was chugged down the edge of the flat in the background on falling water. There's no uncertainty when a red grabs a bait--the cork disappears instantly.

Sardines are plankton eaters, like most of the basic baitfish of the sea, rapidly converting the minute organisms in the water into usable protein that forms the base of the food chain for predators. But sardines also eat bits of fish flesh when they can find it, and this makes it easy to attract them with chum.

The common chum mix is canned jack mackerel combined with a can of oil-mix sardines, plus enough whole wheat bread to make a pasty mix. Some anglers like to add a few drops of anise oil, molasses or other scent, but this is probably gilding this rather odoriferous lily.

Best area to find sardines is the first flat inside a pass, though they may show up along the beaches or just about anywhere the water is reasonably clear and holding plenty of oxygen. Those susceptible to castnet capture usually reveal themselves by flashing on the surface as they feed, creating a ripple that looks almost like rain.

Small-mesh cast nets with a large diameter and plenty of lead weights work best for capturing sardines. Cast nets are designated by their radius, that is, half the diameter of the open circle, more or less--they don't quite spread out enough to exactly double the radius. So, a 6-foot nominal net might cover a 10 foot circle, and a 10-footer covers maybe 18 feet. It's always

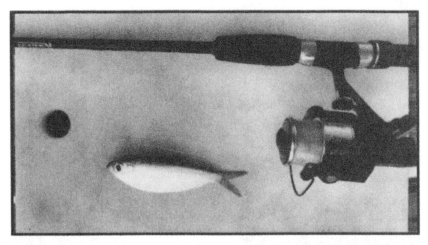

The scaled sardine, also known as "whitebait" in many areas, is one of the deadliest of all redfish baits. They're usually fished with a 1/0 hook through the nose or aft of the dorsal fin.

better to go for the larger net, even though it's more expensive and a bit harder to throw, because it gives you a lot more latitude in entrapping a good pod of fish as all of them explode outward when they see it hit the water. Plenty of weight to pull the net down quickly is also a major factor in an effective net--if it drifts down slowly, a lot of baits will swim out from under it.

Unfortunately, good nets are fairly expensive, starting at $80 and going up to over $150. But they're far superior to the mass-produced jobs you can get for $20 at discount stores. Since you may be spending many hours chasing bait, it makes sense to invest a bit more for a useful tool to catch them.

Sardines are delicate, and require a large live well with rounded corners and a lot of fresh sea water boiling through continuously to stay lively. They're best caught the day they will be used--not many survive overnight.

Sardines are best fished on light-wire hooks in the 1/0 to 2/0 range. They're usually hooked through the clear spot in the nose, the best rig for fishing areas with much tide flow. Hooking just aft of the dorsal works well in calm water , and inspires more dart and flash. With either hook-up, change baits at least every third or fourth cast--a fresh bait catches three times as many fish as a tired one.

The deadliest way to fish sardines, perfected by guide Scott Moore of Cortez, Florida, is to chum a likely hole with them. The baits are squeezed slightly to cause erratic swimming, then lobbed into areas where reds are

42

Tampa Bay guide James Wood brings up a flashing catch. Sardines are caught by chumming with canned mackerel and whole wheat bread over the grass flats. At least 100 per angler are needed for a morning of fishing.

suspected--holes in the flats, oyster bars, outside passes, riprap walls and mangrove points. As the baits go wiggling along the surface, they turn on any red in the vicinity and usually disappear in a boiling strike. You feed them a few free ones, then put out one with a hook in it and you're in business. You can often keep a school in a feeding mood for an hour or more by occasionally flipping out another handful of chum.

Mullet For Lunkers

Mullet are also a prime redfish food, and are found throughout the redfish range from Massachusetts to Florida and around the Gulf to Mexico. The striped mullet is by far the most numerous variety in this area, and make the best baits.

Striped mullet spend much of their time in the estuaries, but between October and January they move offshore in massed schools to spawn. The fry then make their way back into the estuaries to grow up, and as they do they provide a tremendous food resource for reds and other gamefish.

"Finger" mullet, three to six inches long, are outstanding bait for reds. They're not difficult to catch with a castnet, they're durable on the hook, and very active. However, they're tough to keep alive, just like sardines. A large baitwell with a powerful flow-through system is essential to keep them in any numbers. They can't be chummed into range, either, since they're plant eaters--most anglers ease along shallow flats and the edge of passes, or along the beach during the fall run.

Mullet are heavier than sardines, and thus cast better. They also last longer, with a single bait sometimes good for a half-hour of fishing.

With any of the above live baits, the trick in most waters is to fish the offering as naturally as possible. This generally means using no added weight, and casting the bait up-current to allow the natural tide motion to sweep it to the fish. At the end of each sweep, you reel in and cast again, more or less as if you were fishing an artificial. You go through more bait this way than if you just let the bait hang out there downtide, but you also catch a whole lot more fish.

In areas where extra weight is essential to keep the bait in the strike zone--such as in a rip along a beach or when fish are deep around a pier or oil rig--it's a good practice to rig so that the bait still has freedom of motion. You can manage this with a slip sinker in the surf, or by putting the weight at the bitter end of the line and fishing the bait on a long dropper leader around the rigs or piers.

44

Large-diameter nets with plenty of weight are necessary to catch adequate numbers of sardines. Most guides catch lots of extras to use as live chum.

Fish or Cut Bait

All live baits also work well as freshly-cut dead bait, and sometimes a chunk of meat on the bottom will outfish a darting live minnow. This is probably because reds depend as much on their noses as on their eyes to find food, and an oily piece of mullet or shad streaming out juice into the tide attracts them from long distances.

Surf-casters, in particular, do well with cut bait, since they depend on the fish to come to them most of the time. A three-inch mullet fillet fished on a 3/0 hook and anchored with a 2-ounce egg sinker has been the demise of many a redfish along the Atlantic coast.

Most anglers rig their cut baits with slip sinkers, which allows the fish to pick up the bait and swim off with it without dragging the heavy lead. In shallower water, smaller weight or no weight at all is preferred, since the less encumbrance there is on the offering, the more readily the redfish take it.

The one disadvantage with cut bait is that it encourages swallowing the hook, not good in these days of minimal bag limits and catch-and-release fishing. It's a good idea to use de-barbed hooks for easier un-hooking, and to stick with carbon-steel hooks rather than stainless, so that those which go down too deep can be left in place to rust away after the fish is released.

45

CHAPTER 6

THE MAGICAL SPOON

REDFISH MAY NOT BE BORN with gold spoons in their mouths, but they darn sure act as if they'd like to be. There is no other lure, and very few live baits, that will be chased down and slammed so voraciously as these darting, wobbling, shining bits of plated steel. While reds are noted for taking most artificials only when the bait is landed right on the end of their Roman noses, they have what is presently known as an "attitude" when it comes to spoons arriving anywhere on their turf. The gleam of a spoon will bring a redfish charging from 50 feet away in clear water, and they waste no time in blasting it when they arrive.

It's odd that it should be so. Many of the spoons that are most effective were originally designed as lures for freshwater largemouth bass, and particularly for those largemouths found in heavy stands of lily pads where larger, bulkier plugs could not travel.

But these same lures, when cranked across the broad, open shallows of the salt flats, put out a combination of flash and action that triggers something in reds, where ever they are found.

Long Range Lures

One of the big advantages of spoons, other than their remarkable attraction for redfish, is their range. No other lure is so compact and streamlined as the spoon, so no other lure can be thrown so far with so little effort. A 1/2 ounce spoon will fly 15 to 25 feet further than a plastic or wooden plug of similar weight, farther even than a leadhead jig. That extra distance not only means you can reach more fish from a given boat position or wading spot, but more importantly, it means you can stay farther away from your intended victims. This is growing increasingly important these days, when many redfish have been caught and released several times before

47

they reach puberty. They're becoming smarter and more wary, and anything that helps you keep them from suspecting there's a designing angler in their vicinity is sure to result in more strikes.

Shallow Stuff

Though spoons are dense and allow great casting distance, paradoxically they are also capable of "planing" along in only inches of water, something that most heavy lures can't do at all. The design of most spoons allows them to gain lift from passing through the water as you reel, sort of like a miniature slalom ski, and this permits some to run in as little as an inch of water effectively. And, because of the weedless hook design of most, they can scoot across the occasional dry spots without getting stuck or collecting debris that will ruin their action.

Fortunately, these spoons like to run in the same water where redfish go when they're in the mood for chow. This happy juxtaposition results in grins on the faces of spoon fishermen all over the southeast coast, so long as water temperatures on the flats are adequate to keep the fish happy.

Rigging For Spoon Fishing

Most spoons for reds weigh 1/3 to 1/2 ounce, a bit much for light tackle. Whippy rods and lines testing 6 pounds may be just the thing for flinging a shrimp or a sardine, but they're too wimpy for tossing metal. In order to take advantage of the range inherent in the spoon, you need a stiff, light graphite rod, about 6 1/2 feet long in baitcasting, 7 feet long in spinning, with a two-handed grip that will really allow you to apply some leverage on the cast.

The line should be 8 to 10 pound test for spinning, 12- to 14-pound test for baitcasters. (I know, Mr. Walton, you can land a 20-pound red on a thread of horsehair. But see, you don't need the heavy line to fight the fish--you need it to keep the spoon from sailing off into the next county when you put the muscle to it on the cast. A spoon's weight will pull a lot of line, but the moment you try to get it started, the stress can be too much for ultra-thin monos. If you over-do it, your $4 spoon still goes just as far, but the line won't go with it.)

Leaders

You'll probably want to use a shock leader for reds, though it doesn't have to be particularly heavy stuff unless you're in snook country and likely

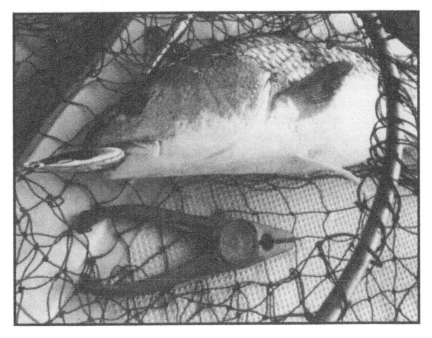

The weedless gold spoon is considered the ultimate redfish lure by anglers in much of the South. It's particularly effective when fish are found over shallow grass or around oyster bars, where the weedguard protects against snagging.

to encounter both reds and linesiders in the same water. Though reds have no teeth, they do have rough "crushers" in the back of their mouths, and should a lure get swallowed (we hope it doesn't, but it happens now and then) the leader prevents a cut-off. The leader gives protection against oyster-encrusted mangrove roots, too, and is stronger at the eye of the spoon, on those that have no split ring.

A barrel swivel is also essential when fishing a spoon because it will prevent line twist. Most guys like to avoid using any kind of hardware between line and shock leader, tying in with a double Uni-knot, Albright Special or Blood Knot so the connection is smooth and snag-free. That's the way to go with most lures, it's true.

But for a spoon, you need the swivel, because all spoons rotate somewhat, and some do it continuously. If there's no swivel to allow that rotation to work itself out, it goes into your line. Before long, you've got a serious bird's nest, or worse, a hidden kink that breaks when a big fish takes off against the drag. It doesn't take a big swivel, though--a size 3, 3/4 of an inch long, is plenty big enough, unless you're fishing for 50-pound monsters in the surf of the Carolinas. The size 3 tests about a hundred pounds in most makes. A size 7, only 5/8-inch long, tests 75 pounds. The smaller the swivel, the less likely it is to put off the fish or to pick up moss.

Thirty-pound test mono makes the best shock leader for spoon fishing. It's heavy enough to prevent abrasion, but not so heavy it affects the lure's action. Buy it in big spools so there's less tendency to coil--and if you're a perfectionist, like Tampa guide Bill Miller, you may want to go to the trouble of cutting off your shock leaders in advance in 18-inch lengths, stretching them out inside a PVC tube, and then boiling them briefly. This makes the leaders perfectly straight and limp. Miller does it so that his tarpon flies ride straight and true, but it works for shock leaders used with larger lures, too. (A tip here--if you use a knot that has to be slid down the standing part of the leader to cinch it tight, such as the Uni-knot loop, slide it down to final position BEFORE drawing it up tight. If you tighten it first, it creates a curl in the leader when it's slid into position.)

The shock leader must be short when you're fishing a spoon--12 inches, after the knots are made and trimmed, is about right. If you make it much longer than that, you'll find yourself reeling the swivel through the tip guide of the rod before you cast in order to get the right pendulum effect on the backcast. It doesn't hurt anything when it goes in, but when it comes speeding back out, it takes the ceramic liner right out of the tip. (Of course, if you're fishing a lighter spoon on a baitcaster, you may have to leave a bit more shock leader hanging, in order to get adequate rod flex on the back-stroke. The farther you hang the lure from the tip, the more it flexes the rod for a given weight.)

The connection of leader to lure should allow for free-swinging action. Many spoons come with a split ring through the eye, solving the problem, but if the one you fish does not, you should tie an end-loop knot such as the Mirr-O-Lure Knot or a cinched-down Uni, to give the lure free motion. This is a very important point in bringing out the action on many spoons.

The Right Spoon For The Job

There are dozens of designs in spoons, and just about all of them will catch reds under the right conditions. However, two of the most widely used are the Johnson Silver Minnow and the Tony Accetta Hobo. The two are similar--both fixed-hook, weedless models--but not identical, and each suits a particular type of terrain best.

This double-spot red took a Johnson Silver Minnow. The spoon is fished on a short leader attached to the running line via a small barrel swivel to prevent line twist.

The Johnson, in the 1/2 ounce size (2 3/4 inches long), is one of the best of all long-distance baits. It's very compact and streamlined due to the soldered construction, and has most of the weight concentrated at the hook end. Thus, it's the spoon to reach for when you have to make a throw out to the limits of your ability to reach spooky fish, or when you're casting upwind.

The Hobo, in the 1/3 ounce size, 2 1/2 inches long, is a stamped metal sheet that has been formed into a curve, with the front end swept up into a slalom ski shape. The hook is attached by a single screw, and a bit of colored feather is tied in to add extra action. The Hobo won't go quite so far as the Johnson. But, it operates better in extremely shallow water because it planes up on top quickly, and it provides lots of action at a lower speed than the Johnson. If you fish spinning gear, you can get plenty of distance with this lighter spoon, though it might be a bit light for most baitcasters.

Sometimes the fish prefer the Silver Minnow, sometimes the Hobo, so it's smart to keep a stock of both. The gold finish is very good in either, though they readily hit chrome, as well.

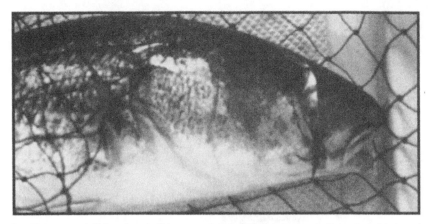

The Hobo spoon is lighter than the Johnson and works better in extreme shallows, though it doesn't cast as far. The spoon features a small red feather on the hook which seems to attract strikes at times.

The new Rebel Arrowhead weedless ·spoon in 1/2 ounce also shows promise, as does the Mepps Size 1 Timber-Doodle. In general, any fixed-hook spoon will work well for reds in the shallows.

Those with free-swinging hooks are also attractive to redfish, but the treble hooks are much more likely to pick up weeds on the flats. You can switch to a large single hook on the split ring, of course, but even then, the dangling hook seems more inclined to catch junk than the fixed hook, weedless models, with or without a wire weedguard.

Incidentally, those weedguards appear to work best if you put a bend in them about an inch in front of the hook, so that the end of the guard is parallel to the barb of the hook and just in front of the tip. This makes the guard more likely to deflect downward when a fish strikes, rather than pinking him in the mouth and causing a quick rejection before you can sink the barb.

Dressings

It's probably not necessary, but many fishermen like to put some sort of chewy treat on the hook of their spoons, as well as on spinnerbaits. A plastic grub tail or a short worm, not more than four inches long, provide added action and perhaps a target close to the barb for the fish to home in on. Pork rind is also useful for this, and one piece lasts all day long. Or, you can add a bit of scent attraction by sticking a piece of Cotee Pro-Bait on the hook. A sliver of cut mullet also works.

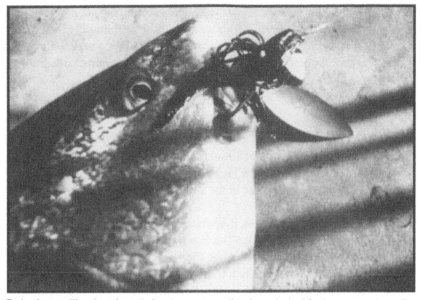

Reds also readily take spinner baits, the same weedless lures devised for largemouth bass. The larger the spinner, the better.

Tuning

Not all spoons are equally effective, even when they are identical in size and model. A slight variation in shape, hook bend, eye or sometimes even the weedless wire can alter the action significantly. What you like best, and what the fish like on a given day, is a matter of experimentation. If you're not getting hit and you know you're on the fish, it doesn't hurt to try some alterations.

One is changing the curve of the spoon. In general, the more a spoon is curved, the more it tends to plane up and to wobble. Less curve makes it run straighter and deeper. Using two pairs of pliers, you can experiment to see if changes in either direction are to the liking of the fish.

Changes in the eye can also considerably alter the way a spoon runs, sometimes adding that something extra that the fish want on a given day. Bend it up to push the nose down, down to push the nose up--but don't bend it far in either direction or it will start to collect weeds.

Sometimes, when reds are settled into holes in thick grass, it's tough to get even a spoon to run past them without snagging. You can help by turning the hook in, just a bit, toward the body of the spoon. This makes it a bit harder to get the hook into a fish, but cuts down considerably on weed problems.

Conversely, when you're in open water and fish are bumping the lure but not getting hooked, sometimes you can improve the connection rate by turning the hook point out slightly. This makes point contact more likely, giving you a chance to get the barb started home.

Spinnerbaits

Spinnerbaits are thought of as exclusively freshwater bass baits, but that's what most people thought about weedless spoons a few years back, too. Now, more and more fishermen are discovering that a large, safety-pin type spinner bait with a gold or silver blade about two inches long is a deadly lure for redfish.

The spinnerbait is weedless, it operates well in water as shallow as a foot, and it can be fished slowly when the fish want it that way, because the big blade provides lift as it moves through the water. It also creates lots of flash and vibration which allow the fish to home in on it, even when the water is murky. The rubber skirts found on most spinnerbaits provide a mouthful for the fish to munch on when they first take hold, too, giving an extra instant to set the hook.

CHAPTER 7

JIGGIN' TRICKS

ALL JIGS ARE EQUAL, of course.

But some jigs are a lot more equal than others.

That's the message that jig makers would have us believe, at any rate--and in a given place at a given time, they can be right. The generic, quarter-ounce lead-head with a soft-plastic grub or shrimp-style body is good for a lot of things, but maybe not the best choice for all situations. The guys who know when to tie on a variation of this most versatile of all lures generally manage to go home with more than an equal share of the redfish.

The Right Weight

Carrying a selection of head sizes is essential to being ready for whatever the day might bring. For the inshore flats guy, the variety ought to start with 1/8 ounce sizes, and include 3/16's, 1/4, 3/8, and 1/2 ounce. This gives you what it takes to fish any depth from one foot on down to 30 feet under most conditions, and to take on anything from 12-inch rat reds to 50-pound bulls.

If you do your fishing around the offshore oil rigs of Louisiana, or sling hardware off the beach at Hatteras, some more robust jigs are called for, starting at the 1/2 ounce size and going up in 1/2 ounce steps to at least 3 ounces. This gives adequate weight to reach depths greater than 30 feet, even with strong tides running. For the surfcaster, the extra weight is essential for long casts. (Your jig box may need wheels, but you'll be ready.)

However, more weight doesn't simply mean a bigger lure. Heavier jigs behave differently than lighter ones, and that difference can make or break you. (I know, they told you in high school that a feather and a marble fall at the same rate--in a vacuum. In water, there's a considerable difference.)

The lower the weight in relation to the bulk, the slower the jig sinks. Light heads with bulky bodies sink slowly, while heavy heads with stream-

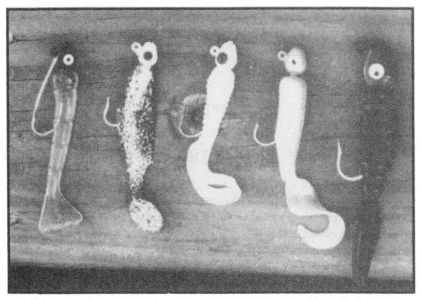

Jigs come in a variety of tail styles to imitate varying live baits. The paddle tail and shrimp tail versions imitate shrimp, while the three swimmer tail models in the center imitate small baitfish.

lined bodies sink rapidly. And most of the time, the slower, more lifelike fall of a lighter jig is more attractive than the dead-weight plummet of a big, heavy head. For species like reds, trout and snook in shallow water, heads in the 1/8 to 1/4 ounce range are the ticket 90 percent of the time.

However, sometimes the fish seem to want a lure that MOVES. In jigs, one of the ways to add action is to increase the weight, resulting in a very rapid fall. The extra weight also allows for a very rapid retrieve while still keeping the lure fairly deep. Light-weight jigs quickly plane up on top when you really turn the crank. Thus, if you're after fish that are active but deep, you need more lead than normal in the jig, though you may not want a proportionately large tail for smaller fish. Move up to a 3/8 head from a 1/4, while keeping the same body size, and you have a lure that sinks much faster, or stays deep at higher retrieve speeds--both effective for deep fish in a high-current area.

Tails, You Lose

The "tails" or bodies of jigs are now almost universally made of soft plastic, designed to make the fish hang on long enough for the angler to set the hook. The tails last through a couple of fish and then are replaced. (A new "Hard-Body" design, with a hard plastic tail that never needs replacing, also catches fish. But a lot of anglers believe the softer body makes the fish hang on longer, giving them an extra edge.)

Plastic tails come in a bewildering array of styles, colors and sizes, and all of them catch fish at times. The basics, though, are the simple paddle-tail or grub design that theoretically looks like a shrimp, the curly-tail swimmer with a rippling tail that maybe looks like an eel, and the shad-type swimmer with a bulbous tail that makes the back end vibrate rapidly--the famed shad or "Cocahoe minnow" imitation. There are literally hundreds of variations on these basic themes, and thousands of colors schemes.

It makes sense to carry a dozen of each of the three basic designs, at least, in light and dark colors. The brownish shade known variously as "motor oil" or "root beer" seems to work everywhere, particularly in darker water, while gold fleck or silver fleck is the favorite in clearer areas. Other popular colors include white, yellow, chartreuse and pink.

There's no question that soft plastics are great jig bodies in most places and for many species. But other materials often work equally well, and are sometimes superior.

If you want longevity, it's hard to beat a nylon body. A single nylon will outlast a dozen plastic tails--although, when the nylon finally does go, you have to put on a whole new jig. The sheen and the "flowering" action of nylon tails seem particularly attractive when the fish are chasing small baitfish, and these days some companies tie in some Mylar strips to add flash and make them even better.

And bucktail, now seen infrequently on the saltwater scene, has a special advantage in that it adds both bulk and flotation to a jig. A thickly-tied bucktail on a lightweight head can greatly slow the fall of a jig, or make it buoyant enough to scoot across a grass flat where plastic jigs will dig in. The natural hair won't stand the chomp of toothy fish, but for reds, it can be superior at times.

Hook Size

A 1/4 ounce jig can be built on any hook size from a 6 to a 3/0. Mold it on the short-shank 6 and you've got a crappie jig. Mold it on a forged 3/0 and you can catch a 100-pound tarpon with it. For reds, you want something in between. The idea is to match the hook size to the tail and to your tackle, rather than exclusively to the size of fish you hope to catch.

This Cotee Shad has a flexible tail that vibrates rapidly as the lure is hopped through the water. Note how the plastic body lies straight on the hook--essential to avoid line twist when the lure is retrieved.

For example, if you're fishing light spinning gear in the backcountry for the typical inshore red between 4 and 10 pounds, you probably want a tail between 3 and 5 inches long--the shorter if you're a Floridian, the longer if you're a Texan. (This says less about fish preferences--or the psyche of anglers in the two states--than it does local custom. Or does it?)

But if you fish the short tail, a 1/4-ounce head with a smaller hook, in the 1 to 1/0 range, will be just right. The lighter wire-hook is a lot easier to drive home with that thin, stretchy mono than would a bigger, thicker hook.

If you use bigger tails, on the other hand, you need a bigger hook to prevent masking the barb with the body. You might still want a light wire, to help in setting the hook, if you're fishing 8-pound-test or less. Sometimes you can find long-shank jig hooks of light wire molded on some sizable heads, and these are the ticket for the light-tackle angler. Bubba Jigs of Tampa, FL, among other makers, makes a nice long-shank light wire head.

Alternatively, you might go to somewhat heavier tackle. The idea is to put out a matched offering that takes advantage of the right hook size and wire size in combination with the strength of the line and the stiffness of the rod.

(An aside here: debarbed hooks make it easier to release fish un-harmed, and also make it much easier to hook them. The barb is the major

This 10-pound Louisiana red took a 1-ounce jig dropped down a jetty shore near the mouth of the Mississippi River. Lighter jigs would not hit bottom in the rapid current, and caught no fish.

obstruction to hook set, and can be a real problem with light mono. If you crush the barb or file part of it away, the hook goes home a lot easier. True, you will occasionally lose a fish , but in these days of so much catch-and-release, debarbing makes sense. Surprisingly, no manufacturer has thus far caught on to building lures on barbless or reduced-barb hooks, but it's a simple operation to flatten the barb on any jig with a squeeze of your needle nose pliers.)

Head Design

A jig is a jig is a jig, right?

Not necessarily, according to the experts.

Jig connoisseurs will quickly tell you, as they have me, that designing a successful jig head is part art, part alchemy.

Some, like tech-engineer-turned-jig-maker Steve Marusak of Cotee Jigs in Port Richey, FL, believe in designing the head so that the lure swirls and swims on the fall. Marusak has invested several hundreds of thousands of dollars into precision injection molding equipment that make every one of his jigs exactly like every other one down to a thousandth of an inch. Every honed hook sits in that molded head exactly like very other hook. And the result is remarkable consistency of action, and a devoted following of anglers who will fish no other jig but Cotee.

Other jig makers pour their heads out of lead pots in their garage, with quality control that is more quality anarchy. But even the products from these shops catch fish decently in seasoned hands.

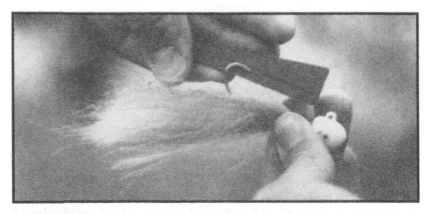

Whatever the jig, it's smart to sharpen the point before use. Many experts also flatten the barb, particularly on large hooks, so that they can be driven home more easily on light lines.

Some makers swear they want nothing to do with any sort of gyration, insisting that a jig should not have a mind of its own, and that a straight drop catches more fish. Some want their jig to hang perpendicular to the line, some at 45 degrees.

A few general observations, and then I'll stay clear of this fray:

1. Knife- or butterbean-shaped heads sink faster than round or flat heads, so if you want to get deep with minimal weight, choose accordingly.

2. Bullet or needlenose heads troll better than round heads, with less tendency to spin or wander, and those with the hook eye further forward generally troll better than those with the eye amidships.

3. For vertical jigging, those with the eye centered in the top of the head seem to sink straighter, stay on target better. Bullets, butter beans and round heads work best.

4. Flat heads or skimmer heads like those used by bonefish anglers in the Florida Keys are also effective on redfish and other species found in minimal depths. They plane along over the bottom grasses rather than digging in.

5. There are now a few "floating jigs" on the market, with a foam head instead of lead. These allow fishing in extreme shallows, and are also effective in deeper water when the fish are looking up. They can be popped and skittered just like a surface plug. Twelve Fathom Jigs in Largo, FL., is among the makers.

6. Tandem rigs are a unique alternative that at times seem to catch fish

turning down singles. The lures, connected by 25-pound-test leader or thereabout, are each smaller than the usual, yet the pair produces casting weight equal to a larger jig. Sometimes, that's what the reds want. Love Lures of St. Petersburg, FL., makes a particularly appealing combo, as does Cotee and other makers.

Jigging Techniques

With jigging, as with so much in life, making the right moves at the right time is everything.

Some anglers are naturals, some never get it right.

The basic idea of a jig is that it can imitate a lot of different critters, depending on what you decide to do with it. Swim it along bottom, barely twitching it, and it's a crab or an eel. Slow hop it in 12-inch leaps and it's a shrimp. Bigger hops near bottom and it's a panicked shrimp. Bigger, faster hops near the surface and it's a baitfish.

This versatility is the reason that jigs work so well in so many places and on so many species, including redfish.

The basic redfish retrieve in shallow water with a light head is a slow rise and fall, generated by raising the rod tip about six inches, then allowing it to drop back as you take up slack. The idea is to match your speed to the water, so that the jig flirts with bottom at the lower end of the cycle, but doesn't actually touch unless the bottom is open mud or sand. (In such an open area, it's good to make solid contact, stirring up little puffs of mud--reds seem to think this is a crab or a shrimp on the move.)

A second basic retrieve is the straight crank, best with curly-tail or shad-tail swimmers. The idea here is the same as with a spoon, to let the built-in action of the tail do the attracting. Crank just fast enough so that the lure runs a few inches above the bottom or the grass.

For deeper water, a variation of slow-hopping sometimes works best. The trick is to make a much larger motion with the rod, a couple of feet at least, to make the lure jump upward in the water column. Feel it back down, allowing it to fall but maintaining slight tension on the line as you wind. Swim it along bottom a few feet, then hop it upward again. The upward hop attracts the attention of nearby reds. The strike may come on the fall, or on the swim.

In vertical jigging, the upward pump is emphasized even more, jumping the lure four feet or more, then feeling it back down. Don't simply let the line go slack on the fall or you'll miss a lot of fish--it's essential to maintain just a light back-pressure so that you can feel the take.

Cotee "Pro Bait" lure flavoring can be a big asset in murky water. This Mississippi River fish, like more than 40 others taken in a June morning, took the tipped jig while ignoring identical lures that were not tipped. Apparently the fish could not find the jigs in the muddy water without added scent.

And sometimes, in shallow water with active fish, you can turn a sinking jig into a surface lure with good results. Hold the rod high, use a light jig, and retrieve steadily as you twitch and hop the lure just under the surface. This is a good trick over grass that makes a normal jigging retrieve impossible, and will get the jig through some areas where a spoon would have problems. (It's not a bad idea to carry a few jig heads with nylon weedguards for such situations, by the way--Cotee makes some good ones.)

Some anglers have learned to twitch their jig up on top the instant the lure lands, creating a flutter of quick motion, and then allow it to sink. That brief flutter on top often draws fish from afar.

With floating jigs, of course, you can follow the standard patterns of fishing floating plugs, which we'll cover in the next chapter--the basic pattern is an imitation of a wounded baitfish, with plenty of quick twitches followed by moments of hesitation.

Tipping

Redfish, like waiters, are fond of the practice of tipping.

In the redfish case, however, the "tip" is a bit of scent added to the hook to make the jig extra toothsome.

Jigs are one of the few lures which can handle a bit of natural bait on the hook and not lose most of their action. But you have to be modest in the tip-- standard policy among outdoor writers, in any case.

For small jigs, a bit of shrimp, fresh mullet or pinfish about the size of a pencil eraser is all it takes, and more is not better. The larger the tip, the more it interferes with the action of the jig and changes the appearance. The idea is to get just a bit of scent on the lure, not to feed the fish.

Which brings us to artificial lure scents. Cotee Pro-Bait and the new "Natural Bait" seem to have a corner on the market, with small, tough tips that last a long time and are deadly for most species of marine fish, including reds. Pro-Bait incorporates chemically compounded shrimp scent into a tough foam and cloth matrix, while the fleshy-feeling Natural Bait is actually made up of 25 percent shrimp, fish, or squid and is totally edible. It's a deadly mix for tipping a jig, or fished alone on a jig head.

Spray-on scents can also help at times, though you have to re-coat the jig every couple of casts. (The easy way is to put the scent in a cup, and drop your jig in there every second toss.)

There are times when reds won't take jigs, or when there are better lures than the jig for fishing a particular type of water, but for versatility, you can't beat a box full of lead-heads.

CHAPTER 8

PLUGGING ALONG

Most redfish caught on plugs are caught by accident by anglers fishing for trout, snook or other species, but baitfish-imitating plugs, both floaters and sinkers, are extremely effective for all reds beyond their first year of life. Reds eat primarily shrimp and minnows when they're small, but large baitfish become increasingly important as they get big enough and fast enough to catch them. Sardine-sized fish are among the major diet items of the typical inshore red in the 4- to 12-pound class.

Though the largest drum are thought to eat mostly large crabs according to researchers with the North Carolina DNR, even these giants still gulp down plenty of striped mullet, pinfish, croaker and other smaller baitfish. (Interestingly, the big guys also eat lots of sand dollars and sea cucumbers too, according to the biologists--but nobody has come up with a sea cucumber lure so far!)

Sinking Plugs

Reds are most readily caught on slow-sinking plugs. Their underslung mouth makes it difficult for them to strike at lures over their heads, so plugs that drop down to their level make an easier target.

The slow-sinkers are also easier to fish in the shallow waters where reds are found around much of the Intracoastal Waterway and the estuaries of the Southeast. A lure that sinks to 2 to 3 feet at normal retrieve speed will work best in most waters, though when the fish drop off into channels and holes, much heavier lures capable of dropping down to 10 or 15 feet will be more effective. In water deeper than 15 feet, lead-head jigs or live bait are a better choice than plugs most of the time.

Among the lures which work well when reds are shallow are the Bagley Finger Mullet, the 52M and 38 M MirrOlure, the Hot Flash and the

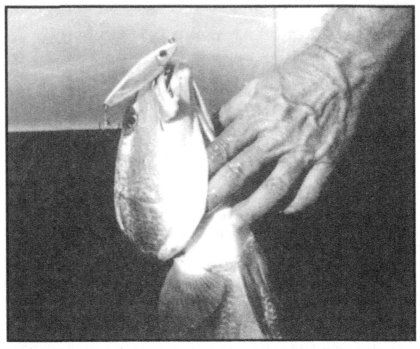

Sardine--imitating lures like this MirrOlure M28 are very effective for redfish throughout their range. The lure is fished in short, sharp jerks to imitate a wounded minnow.

"floating" Rat-L-Trap, which actually dives a few inches under the surface on retrieve. Trader Bay's teak pinfish imitations are also effective, especially for big reds.

All of these lures are best fished in short, erratic hops that cause them to dart and flash like injured baitfish. In general, it's better to fish the lures slowly for reds, allowing a second between twitches as you take up slack with the reel. This keeps the lure close to the bottom and also gives reds plenty of time to make up their mind to take.

It's not exactly a plug, but it's not a jig either, so we'll include here the remarkably life-like shrimp imitation called the D.O.A. This weedless plastic lure looks almost exactly like a live shrimp as it is cranked slowly through the water. It sets upright, and has a pair of weedless hooks snuggled up to the flanks. Various weights can be slipped into a pocket in the body to control depth. It's a unique concept in lures, and it has proven extremely deadly on not only reds but most other inshore gamefish.

66

The Rat-L-Trap is also a great sardine imitation, and it adds sound to the flash and vibration to help the fish locate it. Both floating and sinking versions are available.

With both the slow-sinkers and the D.O.A., you can't fish too slowly to catch reds. Even when you think the bait is doing nothing, it's sinking slowly, and just that motion is enough to draw a strike many times. If you're not catching fish, slow down, most lure-makers advise.

Reds readily take topwaters, even though their underslung mouths sometimes make it tough for them to grip a floater. Topwaters work especially well when drifted under mangroves that hang too low for an effective cast.

Deep Runners

There are times and places when slow-sinkers won't get to redfish, as when they gather deep around the oil-rigs off the Louisiana delta or settle into ship basins during Florida cold fronts. At these times, plugs that really get down are essential.

Diving crankbaits do the job, though few saltwater anglers make use of them. Big jawbreakers like the Mann's Stretch 20+, the Bomber 24A, Rebel Spoonbill Minnow and similars can be trolled deep, going further down the more line you let out.

Weighted plugs that sink of their own accord are also effective, particularly during cold weather when the fish are inactive and don't want to chase a fast-wobbling crankbait. Sinkers like the Rat-L-Trap and the 65M

The Bangolure SP-5 is a great needlefish imitation, and reds can't seem to turn it down. The lure is jerked under, then allowed to flash back to the top on slack line.

MirrOlure can be put on the bottom in water 20 feet deep or more, then worked with slow flits and twitches of the rod. It's a great way to catch lunker winter trout, too, and they often settle into the same holes where reds are found.

Jigging spoons--chromed lead weighing an ounce or more or a thick slice of stainless steel such as the Hopkins line--are also effective in these situations. The lure is dropped straight to the bottom, then flicked upward a foot or two. The rod is lowered just fast enough to keep slack out of the line, but not slowly enough to interfere with the fluttering, glittering fall. Most strikes come on the drop, and are announced by the slightest twitch of the line.

Topwaters

Reds aren't really built to eat baits on top of the water because of the underslung position of their mouths, but they do it a lot anyway. The trick for them to get hold of a floater is to come at it from straight below, so that they can tilt back and inhale it. This can sometimes be difficult in extremely shallow water, as IGFA world-record holder David Fairbanks recounts.

"We were fishing water less than a foot deep on Sarasota Bay when I saw a nice red approaching my floater. He boiled on it three times, but he didn't get hooked. Then, the lure went over a little pothole where the water was about two feet deep. The red dropped into that, went to the bottom, and then came back straight up and gulped the lure down. I think that's why reds so often seem to "miss" a shallow water bait. They actually are on target, but they just can't get hold of it until it gets over a little deeper water."

It would be tough to find a topwater lure that a redfish won't try to eat. But there are favorites. Among the floater-divers are the number 11 Rapala, the Bangolure, the Redfin, the Rebel F-20, the Bill Norman Jerkbait, and the Storm Thunderstick.

All of these lures usually work best when they're jerked under, then allowed a bit of slack so that they pop back to the surface without too much forward motion. The idea is to give a quick, darting flash that attracts the eye of the fish, without moving it away from him. The floater-divers don't create a lot of surface commotion, which makes them a good choice for calm days, confined or shallow waters, or very clear water.

Prop baits make more of a fuss, and are thus better choices for rough or murky water, or for large, open flats where they can be used to toll in reds from considerable distances.

Among the best are the Bangolure SP-5, the MirrOlure 5M, the Devil's Horse, and the Baby Torpedo. All of these except the 5M MirrOlure and the Devil's Horse have only a tail spinner, and a lot of anglers like to take the front spinner off both on the theory that it's inclined to wrap up in the line and spoil the action. The 5M sits a bit more tail-down with the front spinner gone, too, which slightly changes the sound when it's jerked through the water. Reds, as well as snook and trout, respond well.

Prop baits are generally worked in a rhythm similar to that with the floater-divers, allowing slack between each twitch so that the bait very slowly staggers across the surface, rather than skittering along rapidly. Many anglers get into a jerk, jerk-jerk, pause routine that reds seem to like particularly, with the strikes often coming on the pause.

Stickbaits have no action of their own, but when danced along the surface in the hands of an expert like world-record-holder David Fairbanks, they come alive.

Chuggers also catch some reds, though probably fewer than other surface lures. These are flat or cup-headed lures which give a "bloop" like a plumber's helper when they're jerked through the water. Examples include the Lucky 13, the Rebel Pop-R and the Dalton Special, which combines a tail spinner with the popping head. They're very noisy plugs, best used in very rough or murky water most of the time.

The lures are worked with an abrupt jerk, which causes a loud splash that sounds a lot like a fish hitting on top. You then follow up with several small twitches, just enough to make the lure dance, trying to entice any fish that may have approached on hearing the first bloop. If there's no strike after a few seconds, the plug is jerked again.

Finally, there are "stick" baits which have no action of their own. These work in both smooth and rough water, and depend on rapid, erratic action to draw impulse strikes as they pass over the fish.

The Zara Spook and the smaller Puppy Spook are the classic examples. These lures are fished in a zig-zagging pattern known as "walkin' the dog" by many Southern anglers, and they draw some fearsome strikes--though the larger model often is missed by small and medium fish. The trick in working the Spook is to keep the rod tip low and work it in a series of sharp, six-inch twitches with momentary slackening between to allow the lure to work back and forth. It's a tiring lure to work, but very effective at times.

Other stick baits such as the 95M MirrOlure and the Slap-Stick float with their tail down, and the noise out of the water. When the plug is jerked, the tail rises and flashes before settling again. These are good baits for all types of water conditions.

A unique new soft plastic needlefish imitation marketed as the "Jerk Worm" and the "Slog-Go" has also proven deadly on reds. It was originally sold as a bass lure, but reds can't leave it alone. The lure is rigged most often on a single 5/0 hook, and then jerked and twitched through water 1 to 2 feet deep. It darts and drives and splashes like an injured needlefish and seems appealing to reds of all sizes, including the monsters. Guide Shawn Foster of Cocoa Beach has landed fish to 50 pounds on the lure. Foster says it also works well in slightly deeper water when rigged with a sliding sinker like a plastic worm, or Carolina-rigged with a the weight separated from the lure by a swivel. It's totally snag-free, a plus around oysters and mangroves.

Fine-Tune Your Plugs

Seemingly identical plugs don't all work the same, so it's wise to carefully check the action of a new lure the first time you put it in the water. If you luck into one with that special action the fish like, treasure it and try to see what it is about that particular lure that makes it work.

All your lures will work better if you tie them on with a loop knot, which allows them to swing freely on the leader. A split-ring swivel also serves this function.

Tie on your lures with a loop-knot so that they swing freely. This greatly improves the action of most lures.

Colorwise, most of the metallic finishes work, with chrome and gold the most popular. Green, blue or black backs help to imitate the natural baitfish patterns. If you fish after dark, some black or dark purple lures may be more effective than the brighter hues. These same colors also work better in tannin stained water, where most of the baitfish are darker colored.

Sharpen all hooks regularly, and flatten the barbs with pliers. This makes it easier for the hooks to go home, and also makes it easier to back them out on fish you intend to release.

Finally, wash your used plugs down with fresh water and allow them to dry before putting them back in your tackle box. If you put a salty lure in your box, even the best hardware will eventually start to corrode, and the salt is like cancer, spreading its vapors to anything in the box that can rust or corrode. Drop the lures in a bucket as they are used, and then when you finish the day, add a few drops of dish soap and fresh water, give them a quick rinse, and let them drip dry on a paper towel. Your old favorites will have an unlimited lifespan with this treatment.

CHAPTER 9

FLY-RODDING FOR FLATS REDS

IT'S BEEN SAID that a fly rod, like a golf club, is "an instrument ill-conceived to its purpose".

There are, after all, far easier ways to catch most fish most of the time than by flailing away at them with an underweight bull whip. But a growing cadre of anglers around the southeast are learning that redfish, like tarpon, have a peculiar weakness for the delicate offerings that can be presented with the long rod. In fact, there are days when the fly-rodder can put it on the hardware slingers with their baitcasters and spinning rods.

And those who do will tell you that they have more fun per fish, doing it.

One such angler is Pete Greenan of Sarasota. Greenan began flyrodding up in Yankee country when he was still in knee pants, and never gave up his affinity for the gear even after he moved to Florida some 20 years ago. These days, he guides reds, trout and snook from Sarasota Bay to the Everglades, and he encourages all his clients to bring along their flyrods.

"Reds are perfect flyrod targets," says Greenan. "They're abundant thanks to conservation, they're bigger than the average bonefish, and they're found in knee-deep water half the time. Plus, you can't get a shrimp pattern anywhere near them without getting bit. What's not to like?"

Tampa tarpon guide Bill Miller has also homed in on reds as the best of off-season targets for his fly-rodding clients.

"You don't have to be able to throw a hundred feet to catch reds, and they're a lot less spooky than some flats species like bones and permit," he notes. "Plus, you don't have to drive to the keys to connect. We've got some of the best fishing for big reds along the west coast right now that we've had in 20 years."

Other west coast guides who have tuned in to redfish on the fly include Paul Hawkins and Russ Sirmons at St. Petersburg, Ray DeMarco at Anna Maria Island, James Wood at Terra Ciea, and Earl Waters at Homosassa. Waters was one of the west coast pioneers of shallow water redfishing with the fly 10 years ago.

"Most anglers love sightfishing once they get into it," Waters observes, "and there's no better target than reds in clear water. They tail, they push water, and they make a big, obvious target. It's a great way to get started in saltwater fly fishing."

Prime west coast flyrodding waters extend roughly from Crystal River on the north to Marco Island on the south. North of this area the inshore flats turn coffee black with tannin stain from the big rivers, while to the south the murk of Everglades rivers is less welcoming to sight fishermen--though there's good flyrodding on the outside, in the flats of Florida Bay, and anglers there have been aware that reds are a likely target for flies for years. You can also spot reds in the stained but clear headwaters of the Everglades creeks in late winter.

Winter Flyrodding

A trip I made to Charlotte Harbor not long ago with Pete Greenan is a case in point. It was a miserable, blustery January cold front morning, so nasty that I called Pete at 4 a.m. and asked if he actually wanted to give it a try despite the flag-snapper whistling past the windows.

"Yeah," said Pete. "They'll bite. Bring your waders."

Think duck hunting, I told myself. You've done dumber things than this to go duck hunting. Why not redfishing?

A little after sunrise, we piled into Pete's flats skiff at Eldred's Marina on the Boca Grande Causeway and headed south. I pointed out to Pete that nearly all the water in Charlotte Harbor had done likewise, the bay being blown nearly dry by the ripping northeast wind on a falling tide.

"Yeah," he grinned, his cheeks rosy through his beard. "Beautiful, ain't it?"

We wound our way back into the mangroves through water where a Jeep would have been a better vehicle. I fish the area frequently, but there were bars sticking out of the water that I had never seen before on the lowest of spring tides. In fact, so much water had left that the mangrove-lined bays had broken into a series of shallow pools surrounded by exposed grass and mud. There was no floating any sort of a boat in this water, so we staked out,

76

Reds are easy flyrod targets when they invade waist-deep water. Most fly-rodders prefer to wade to allow a close, low-profile approach to their targets.

wiggled into waders and slid over the side, eight-weight rods in hand, weedless brown shrimp patterns at the end of the nine-foot leaders.

Yuck.

Muck.

Considerable mud, especially wherever the grass grew. I quickly learned to walk where the white sand marked a path, because bottom was hard in those areas. Dark or grassy bottom meant tough walking. (You must have suspenders for this work, because otherwise the suction of the mud will have you constantly fighting to keep your waders up.)

The "deep" water remaining in the basins was perhaps 30 inches, with 18 inches about the average.

Pete pointed out that a trough of slightly deeper water runs down the edge of each grassy bar, just after the bottom falls toward a sandy area, and that fish often settle into this trough on extreme low water.

"If you don't see fish, blind-cast the trough," Greenan advised. "Keep moving, and eventually you'll hit one, or spot one tailing that you can throw to."

Pete said that even in the diminutive world of the blown-out tidal basins, reds tend to congregate around natural ambush areas such as grass points or the channels between one basin and another, so we threw to those areas with extra care.

The first basin produced only casting exercise--no fish sighted, no fish hooked. We slogged across a mud flat, pushing up clouds of wading birds ahead of us, and dropped into the next basin.

On about the third cast, Pete went on point, stripped his fly a couple of quick hops, and slapped the barb home when he saw a seven-pounder flare open his white mouth and inhale.

The fish didn't understand the problem at first, and swam right up to Greenan's legs. When it saw the "mangrove" move, it got the idea and headed for the horizon, taking all the flyline and part of the backing with it. Fishing a 10-pound tippet, Pete had no choice but to let it go.

He got three good runs from the fish, each followed up with considerable pumping and winding and staggering around the basin after the fish, trying to avoid the sucking mud, me trailing with the camera. By the time the redfish was worn out, so were we.

But by the time he had been unhooked and revived, we were ready for another.

I spotted a brown bomber crossing a white patch of sand, left to right, about 40 feet out. I shot the fly ahead of him, stripped twice, and saw him home in on it, rush forward, and gulp it down.

When I set the hook, this one, like Pete's fish, simply shook his head and swam in a slow circle, chewing, apparently trying to kill the feisty crustacean

78

Reds sometimes prowl water that's only ankle deep. They're readily spotted "tailing" in such locations. A long, soft delivery is required to avoid spooking fish in these depths.

that had barbed him. But when I got the line on the reel and began to pump, he went bananas. He shot off in a straight-line run that took all the fly line and at least half the backing, a sprint of close to a hundred yards. It wasn't as fast as a bonefish, but there was more authority.

By the time I had the 30-incher in hand 10 minutes later, my wrists and forearms were aching and I no longer felt cold at all.

It went like that for the rest of the morning, with a fish popping up about every 15 minutes as we eased across the flats. We didn't see the big, tight schools sometimes found in the area on higher water, but the fish that were there were willing to eat so long as we got the fly to them before they saw us--and most didn't spot us until they were 20 feet away. The soft drop of the fly didn't spook a single fish.

Greenan said that after a cold front, flyrodding the area is usually best from about 10 a.m. to 3 p.m., the hours when the sun warms the flats and makes the fish more active. In moderate winter and spring weather, the fish may bite all day--but they're often easiest for the fly-rodder to find on low water, when the available habitat is restricted.

On rising water, go with the tide, trying to keep in that prime 12- to 24-

inch water where the reds will be pushing as the flow goes up across the flat. There are plenty of reds in deeper water, of course, but those that are most vulnerable to the fly will be in the shallow stuff, sometimes tipping up to wave their tails in the air to make sure you see them.

Fly-Rodding Florida Reds

Beginning on the north end, prime clear-water flats for tossing a fly to reds exist around St. Martin's Keys between the Crystal and Homosassa rivers, around Chassahowitzka Point, and throughout the needle-rush and mangrove country that stretches south all the way to Hudson. (The Hudson area is still a sleeper, with plenty of fish and not too many flats fishermen.)

Tampa Bay is also prime flyrodding country for reds, with good flats around Bunce's Pass, between Fort DeSoto Park and the Skyway, around all the islands stretching along the south shore from the ICW up to the Little Manatee River, in Cockroach Bay and around Weedon's Island, Double Branch and Rocky Creeks, among other locations.

Sarasota Bay has good redfish waters on both the east and west shores, particularly in the north end.

In Charlotte Harbor, good spots include the mangrove islands and bays on the north side, the east shore of the main harbor, and both shores of Pine Island Sound and Matlacha Pass.

Fly-Rodding Other Waters

Anglers in other parts of redfish range are catching on to the fact that even very large drum will often gulp down a fly. Texas anglers are barbing plenty in the clear waters of the Laguna Madre these days, and there's also fine fly-rodding off Louisiana and Mississippi in the clear flats and the gentle beaches at the Chandeleur Islands.

North Carolina is again the spot for lunkers when it comes to fly-rodding, with the current 12-pound and 16-pound tippet IGFA records taken there. Big one was a true monster, 42 pounds, 5 ounces, taken by Floridian Chico Fernandez in May of 1981. These giants are generally caught by anglers casting to surfacing schools near the passes.

For average-sized reds, eight-weight tackle is best, with weight-forward, floating line to allow fast casts with a minimum of false-casting. Practice until you can quickly and accurately cast 50 feet every time, and you're ready to go redfishing. Being able to throw farther, and to do it into the wind, will get you more fish. But you can get by with 50-footers much of the time.

80

On high tides, reds probe around reeds and mangroves looking for shrimp and crabs. Successful fly-rodders imitate the natural with dark, slow-moving flies.

The usual tapering saltwater leader is needed, starting with a 30-pound butt section five or six feet long, to turn over flies that are tied on size 1 to 1/0 hooks. In snook country, most anglers use a foot of 30-pound-test shock tippet to connect with the fly. Brown or gray shrimp patterns with maribou are popular, as are silvery sardine imitations using Mylar or Flashabou. Some anglers are starting to catch reds on big bucktail poppers like those tied by Jim Stewart, contract designer for Umpqua Feather Merchants, as well.

You don't have to wade to fly fish, of course, but it allows a much closer approach than reds will tolerate from a boat, and also allows easy access to shallow basins that can't be fished at all from aboard.

Reds don't require a lot of action in the fly. Most anglers allow it to sink to bottom, then bring it in with a series of short twitches that barely swim the fly along, about like a shrimp putzing around with nothing on his mind. Reds

81

An eight-weight rod is about right for most inshore redfishing. Weight-forward floating line makes for easy delivery of saltwater streamers and bugs.

are not delicate in the take--they usually arrive in a rush and grab the fly with a boil and a flare of the mouth that's easy to see in the shallows--and they usually hang on plenty long enough for you to sink the barb, as well.

When they're a bit more tentative, they sometimes swim along just behind the fly, their nose inches from it. If you slow down, they'll turn away, but if you speed it up slightly with a couple of quick, short twitches, they'll rush ahead and take most of the time.

For big reds that must be reached at long distances, as when the lunkers school around the North Carolina passes, most anglers opt for 12-weight tackle and super-slick mono-core lines that allow extra long casts. The extra power of these big sticks and the extra capacity of the larger reels helps control these giants as well.

The fly rod may never become your favorite angling tool. It takes some time to master, is subject to the vagaries of wind, and is not the tackle for fishing at long range over unseen fish. But in the right water at the right time, it should be the redfish weapon of choice for the Compleat Angler, 1990's style. If you don't put the long rod to work on reds now and then, you're not playing with a full fishing deck.

CHAPTER 10

WELL-SCHOOLED REDS

HISTORICALLY, REDFISH HAVE NEVER been known as mental giants. They have a tendency to fling themselves suicidally at whatever lure or bait happens to pass under their rounded snouts, often despite the obviously bad results experienced by their schoolmates ahead of them.

But that's starting to change. Reds are beginning to wise up. In fact, they're starting to get downright smart in some areas, at times taking their places beside dock snapper and pier snook as the most frustrating fish in coastal waters.

"It used to be that anybody who could throw a half-ounce gold spoon a hundred feet could go out on the flats and wear himself out catching redfish," says guide Earl Waters of Homosassa. "But it's not like that most days anymore. The fish are still there, but they've gotten a lot harder to catch."

The reason, says Waters and other Gulf Coast guides, is that so many anglers have discovered the delights of shallow water redfishing in the last four years. Tightened management plans and the end of commercial harvest have brought the fish back in great numbers in many states, and that has resulted in a boom in the number of sportfishermen chasing them on the flats. As a result, many reds are now caught and released several times a year. No matter how slow-witted one might be, a 3/0 hook in the mouth finally has to make an impression. Apparently, that's happened to a lot of reds in recent years: the species is definitely becoming harder to catch in clear, shallow water like that found along much of the Gulf Coast and the Intracoastal Waterway of the Atlantic Coast.

So how do you go about fooling these piscatorial post-grads?

Several of the leading guides and anglers between Homosassa and Charlotte Harbor offered the following suggestions:

85

Change Lures

"Avoid the usual lures," suggests noted wildlife artist and redfish expert Don Mayo of Crystal River. "In our area they've seen too much of the spoon. They'll still hit it when things are just right, but a lot of times now, it's better to toss a topwater to them. You can work it slower, you can stop it without getting snagged, and you can leave it right on a fish's nose and bounce it until he has to take."

Mayo and others who fish topwaters like the Bangolure, the 5M and 7M Mirrolure, the Bangolure, the floating Rat-L-Trap and the Tiny Torpedo, among others.

Go Live

"Use the real thing," suggests guide Mike Locklear of Homosassa. "There are times when they won't hit any artificial, no matter how carefully you work it. But if you put out a live shrimp, or a pinfish, or a chunk of fresh mullet, and let that scent drift downtide around the island points and reefs, the fish will come and take it."

Locklear said that live or cut bait often turns up reds "where they ain't", drawing in fish that may be invisible and that would never be caught by those depending on sight-casting an artificial.

Guide Scott Moore, who operates at Cortez and at Boca Grande, suggests offering a bit of sweetener to reluctant reds in the form of live sardines chummed over their lairs.

"They may not be in an eating mood when you pull up if the tide is wrong or if another boat has just passed through," says Moore, "but if you pitch a handful of sardines to them, it wakes them up and gets them thinking about food, and they'll usually take when you put out the baitfish with the hook in it."

Moore catches his sardines by chumming over the grass flats with a mix of wheat bread and canned mackerel, then castnetting them. They're kept alive in a giant, flow-through livewell until needed to turn on reds and snook. He fishes them on light spinning gear, with no weight or float to hinder the bait movement.

Learn The Water

"Learn the water and the tides," says Earl Waters, from Homosassa. "You can go across a point at half-way through a rising tide and not even see a pinfish there. Come back an hour later and there may be a hundred 10-

Catch-and-release redfishing is making many fish smarter. In some areas, the fish disappear anytime a lure lands near them these days.

pound redfish on that spot, all looking for something to eat. They move around quite a bit with the water in this area, and knowing when to be where is a big part of catching fish."

Paul Hawkins guides out of St. Petersburg, Florida. He suggests stealth in the approach as the major reason for his success, catching reds in some of the most intensively fished waters in the state.

"When the water is calm and clear, it's just about impossible to get up to some of the schools I fish in a boat," says Hawkins. "The only effective way to catch them is to get out and wade, so you have a smaller, lower profile."

Fine And Far Away

Hawkins, like Waters and Moore, suggests using tackle that allows you to make long casts, like the new "long cast" spinning reels from Daiwa or Shimano, mounted on rods 7 feet or longer and fully loaded with line testing no more than 8 pounds.

Anglers who can throw 125 feet or more will catch a lot more fish than those who can't break a hundred feet, the guides agree.

FCA leader and guide Russ Sirmons of St. Petersburg also likes the idea of wading to get within range of spooky fish. And, he notes that the delicate presentation possible with a flyrod will sometimes lure reds when the splash of a heavier casting lure spooks them. He agrees, though, that it usually takes a fairly long toss, even with a flyrod streamer, to prevent spooking the fish.

Captain Larry Mendez, one of the top guides at Charlotte Harbor on Florida's west coast, says that fishermen who anchor their boats and let the fish come to them often do better than those who constantly keep moving. Mendez, who runs a shallow-draft Shoalwater boat with a tall tower, uses the excellent visibility from the platform to position his rig in areas where he has sighted fish, then anchors and waits in silence until the reds forget about him. They often take the live sardines he offers.

Don Mayo has also learned that patience pays at times. He notes that one creek he likes near the town of Ozello has no fish at all for most of each day, but during the last hour and a half of falling tide, it loads up with 30-inchers. Mayo gets there before the show starts, ties his boat to a mangrove, and waits for the fish to come to him.

Silence Is Golden

Mayo prefers to keep his boat moving at other times, but notes that it has to be moved silently. Earl Waters agrees, noting that a noisy pushpole scraping across the bottom puts fish off. In fact, Waters has developed a cushioned tip for his graphite pole, and Mayo prefers to use a wood pole because it produces less tip noise and resonance than glass or graphite poles.

Of course, it should go without saying that you can't run your outboard up to a school of reds and catch fish these days, or at least not very often. Many anglers make use of electric trolling motors, however. These are effective, but many who use them warn that the new super-strong 24-volt saltwater models should only be run on the lowest speed as you near the fish-- otherwise, the whirr they give off may be enough to make the school nervous, and nervous reds don't bite.

Avoid The Crowds

Some guides also recommend actively looking for stragglers, rather than seeking out the big schools that have provided so much action in many areas the last few years.

When reds become difficult to catch, experts recommend trying new lures that the fish haven't seen before.

89

Earl Waters of Homosassa was one of the pioneers of shallow-water redfishing in Florida. He recommends learning the tides in a localized area to hit peak feeding periods.

"The schools are easier to find," one guide told me, "but they're easier to find for everybody. That means they get a lot of heat, while that single fish tailing out in the middle of a flat may not have seen a lure in a year. He'll usually eat if you make a quiet approach."

Some also suggested scouting out new areas, rather than hitting the "hotspots" that are becoming very poorly-kept secrets as the location of resident schools becomes common knowledge.

"You may spend half a day just looking for fish in a new area, but if you do luck into reds in a spot that others haven't found, you'll be putting the lure in front of "dumb" fish. It's worth the extra time scouting," says Hudson guide Dennis Royston.

The experts all agreed that fishing weekends is a lot tougher than fishing on weekdays, too.

"These days, there are 10 times as many flats boats as there were five years ago," one told me. "They're all out there running all over the flats from Friday afternoon until dark on Sunday. Fishing takes until Tuesday to get right again. If you have a choice of days to go, pick the middle of the week."

When And How

Several also suggested that, other things being equal, redfish these days are easier to catch early and late, and after dark, than they are during the

Shallow-draft boats make it possible to reach remote backcountry areas where reds see less fishing pressure, but there are more of these boats every year. Experts suggest fishing weekdays, rather than weekends, to avoid the crowds.

brighter hours. So, if you can select weeks when good tides for your area fall during the low light periods, you're putting the odds on your side.

A bit of noise can help, too. Some anglers have learned to make use of vibrating, shot-filled lures like some models of Mirrolure and the floating Rat-L-Trap to get reds looking in the right direction. (The noise-makers have to be used with discretion, though. Some days, the added ruckus seems to be too much for the fish, and they turn away from it.)

Adding scent to sight can also help, some said. By putting a piece of Pro-Bait, a bit of cut shrimp or a sliver of fresh mullet on the hook of a spoon or jig, you can greatly increase the number of strikes from even well-schooled reds.

Bottom line is that you have to pay better attention to all the details if you want to consistently tangle with the educated redfish of the Nineties.

CHAPTER 11

READING REDFISH WATER

THE FLATS ARE AN OPEN book, but only if you know the language. Charts are not of much value for threading your way through the shallows-- it's eyeball navigation, all the way.

Learning to "read" the inshore waters has a mystique about it, cultured by guides who are not in a hurry to have the growing crowd of weekenders discover how to get into and out of those secret spots protected by miles of ankle-deep shallows.

But for the most part, learning to understand what's ahead of you is simply a matter of experience, and of giving your eyes a few advantages to help them see through the surface to what lies below, whether it's down there six inches or six feet.

Choose The Right Time

First comes timing. You can't learn to run the shallows at dawn or dusk. Sunlight, the brighter and the more vertical the better, is essential to seeing what you're about to get into. Thus, when you're learning new water, the only reasonable time to go is during the brightest hours from about 10 a.m. to 3 p.m. After you've had some experience, you can pick up the more subtle hints of changing water color earlier and later in the day, but only if you keep the sun at your back. Timing also comes into play in picking a day when the water is not clouded by a recent storm or heavy rain. When the water is murky, even the saltiest pros have problems--it's no time for an amateur to go punching around. Look for clearer flats, or come back another day.

Go out on rising water, of course. That way, if you stick, you float off in an hour or so, instead of waiting on the tide six to 12 hours with only the 'skeeters for company.

Get High

Secondly, the higher above the surface you can get, the better you can see the bottom. Sitting down at the console gives you almost no visual penetration. Standing is a lot better, enough to allow running most areas if you're careful. But if you have tough water to deal with, you'll find things get a lot easier if you stand on an ice chest as you motor along--tricky, to be sure, but reasonably safe if the chest is roped in place.

If you want the real advantages of elevation, you opt for a tower. This puts your Topsiders about six feet off the deck and your eyes are up there getting an osprey's view. You can see every change in bottom structure and depth, and pick out individual fish--a tremendous advantage when you're scouting new water, and one of the major reasons so many inshore guides insist on running only boats with towers. They're expensive, costing $2,500 to better than $5,000, but many experts say they'd be lost without them.

Gearing Up To Read The Flats

You must have Polarized sunglasses to see through surface glare. Glasses that are not Polarized are useless in flats fishing, though they do give your eyes some protection from the brightness. Most guides prefer glasses with side visors to cut out peripheral glare and appear to clarify the view of the bottom as a result. Most seasoned anglers prefer real glass lenses, rather than plastic, because the plastic tends to scratch quickly due to frequent wipe-downs to remove salt. You need some sort of a safety strap on the glasses, too, so that they don't go sailing away if you turn your head to look aft when you're buzzing along at 40 mph. There are some floating models, which are useful if you do happen to drop them over, and there are also some safety straps that actually float the glasses or whatever they're attached to.

A visored hat is also a must for good vision through the surface. The shadow it provides over your eyes and glasses considerably increases your depth vision. The best have extra long bills, with a dark color on the underside to absorb glare. If you're sun-sensitive, get a hat with a full brim or the front/back bills of the Keys guides hat to protect your neck and ears, rather than just a baseball cap.

The clear water of the shallow flats makes it possible to read the depth ahead once you understand the various color changes. Reds frequently settle into sand holes like this one, surrounded by slightly shallower grass flats.

Water Colors

The beauty of the ever changing carpet of the flats, the incredible variety of hues, is also a map that tells the experienced eye what to expect under the hull--most of the time.

In general, offshore water is very clear, and the deeper it gets, the bluer it gets. Thus the open ocean on a clear day has the color of indigo ink. Inshore water has a bit of sediment, plus fresh water of varying colors in various places, thus looks different in most inshore waters around the U.S. mainland.

In general, deeper inshore waters look dark green, growing paler green as sand shoals rise near the surface. In areas where their are coral heads, such

95

Learning to "read" the inshore waters has a mystique about it, cultured by guides who are not in a hurry to have the growing crowd of weekenders discover how to get into and out of those secret spots protected by miles of ankle-deep shallows.

as in the Florida Keys, these rocky growths look like dark brown patches suspended in the green.

As you move into the really shallow water of the flats, however, most of the green disappears and you begin to see the grass itself, a waving carpet of gray, brown and olive.

In general, water that's deep enough to run with the average flats boat--drawing 12 to 14 inches on plane, trimmed up--looks dark green if the bottom is grassy, light green over sand holes and bars. In water this deep, the bottom does not affect the surface under most tide conditions, so even during the flows, the surface shows no unusual rippling.

In shallower water--maybe too shallow for your boat--the grass begins to look brown, while the sand begins to look yellow or white. (An exception

A tower makes it much easier to see into the water ahead, not only to avoid shallow bars, but also to spot fish. Only wide-beamed boats can handle a tower of this height safely, however.

is deeper sand holes in shallow surrounding grass, such as the depressions found along Florida's west coast. There, dark yellow means somewhat deeper water.)

Very shallow flats also affect the surface ripple, creating herringbone patterns as the water drags across it on tide flows. You may also see the tips of grass coming through the surface on the lower half of the tide. Either of these signals should warn you to stay clear of the area. Wading birds standing ankle deep and exposed crab traps are also warning signs.

In general, one of the safer routes to follow through any flat is the depression that often develops where grass bottom meets sand or mud. These areas are easily visible and sometimes extend for long distances, and the trough is usually as much as six inches deeper than either the mud or the grass.

Also, in every bar you'll find an area where the tides have cut a channel through, allowing the volumes of water from the back country to rush through into the larger bays or the open sea. The idea is to run parallel to the bars until you see one of these cuts, marked by darker water and often by rapid current flow, and use them to jump across the shoal.

97

A few sprigs of mangrove or emergent grass in the middle of a bay should warn of a shallow area--but may also mark a feeding spot for reds.

Preserving The Flats

The impact of boats on the flats is leaping to the top of the conservation heap these days as a point of concern, and some places have already made some grassy areas off-limits for outboards.

If flats anglers don't want to see these sorts of closures become widespread, they'll have to take it on themselves to avoid cutting prop trails through grass--trails that take years to heal if they ever do.

In the days when flats boats were rare, the occasional prop trail caused minimal problems, and may even have been useful as a channel for fish passage. In those days, it was recommended procedure for jumping a flat to blast along with the skeg plowing a furrow, blowing mud and sand aft with a stainless steel prop. But now that there are hundreds of us out there, the trails are becoming broad and deep, and clearly can be a threat to the grass that sustains the fish populations in some areas.

The solution is to avoid running areas where the prop makes frequent bottom contact. Technology can come to the rescue on this, as builders make boats that float ever higher. But it will ultimately be up to the individual angler to know how shallow his boat can run without damaging the grass, and to avoid running in water shallower than that.

You can still penetrate such areas via push pole and electric trolling motor, of course--and there's some evidence, from the "outboard free" flats already in place, that such refuges may provide great fishing because schools of fish will settle into them and remain there if not disturbed by high-speed hulls. But the good old days of cutting your own channel to where ever you want to fish are on their way out.

CHAPTER 12

CATCH-AND-RELEASE REDFISHING

IT USED TO BE UNHEARD OF to put a redfish back, and boats routinely pulled up to the docks with garbage-cans and ice chests stuffed to overflowing with hundreds of them. In fact, the joke at the cleaning tables in those days was that this was "filet-and-release" fishing, with the carcasses tossed into the water for the crabs.

It was too good to last, and it didn't over much of the range. The excess among hook-and-liners combined with the inescapable webs of net fishermen with bigger, faster boats and invisible mono mesh to flatten the fishery in state after state.

Fishery managers finally caught on and passed restrictive laws that are bringing the fish back; the netters are happily on their way out of the fishery in most states, and sensible laws have limited the take of the recreational angler to the amount the local fisheries can hopefully sustain.

But bag limits mean that a lot of fish that are caught have to be released, and if they're not released in good condition, the purpose of releasing them in the first place is defeated.

Reds are among the toughest of saltwater fish, and don't require the delicate handling of spotted seatrout or the mackerels, but they do need some care to get their engines running again after being brought to the boat.

Particularly when they're caught on light tackle which takes many minutes to bring them to the boat, reds are likely to be so tired that they can barely swim when released. In fact, some don't--they simply sink to the bottom, where they flop over on their sides or back. If they're allowed to remain there, they'll die, because it's tough for the exhausted fish to pump enough oxygen over his gills without moving through the water.

To make sure fish destined for release survive, it's best to use tackle in

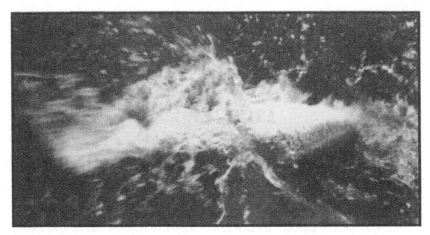

Reds rarely leap, but they provide a powerful battle all the way to boatside. The fish often exhaust themselves, and require artificial respiration for successful release.

the middle ranges, 8-pound-test minimum, so that you can bring them to boatside in a reasonable length of time. Easiest way to get a red aboard without damage is with a landing net, and the best are those with the rubberized webbing, less likely to scrape away the slime coat than hard nylon webs.

Get the fish out and put him down on the deck, so that a flop does not cause a hard fall out of your hands. Remove the hooks--made a lot easier if you've bent down the barbs in advance--take a quick photo if you want one, and then slip the fish back over the side, supporting the head with one hand and gripping the base of the tail with the other.

Pumping Life Into Redfish

Hang on to the tail, and steadily "pump" water through the gills by pushing the fish forward, then pulling it backward about a foot repeatedly. Keep this up until it tries to swim out of your hand.

Then give a final push, out and down, and the fish will usually glide away. Keep an eye on him until he's out of sight, though, because occasionally a fish loses equilibrium at this point and turns over. Sometimes they float, but more often these weakened fish sink to the bottom.

You can often revive these fish by simply reaching out with a rod tip and tapping them on the stomach. The stimulus many times is enough to wake

To revive a fish, hold it by the base of the tail and pump it back and forth through the water. This causes water to flow over the gills, providing oxygen to the bloodstream.

them up and start them swimming. If not, grab the fish again and pump some more until it shows signs of full recovery.

The problems of recovery are greater in warm weather, because the oxygen holds less water then, and the fish are more subject to heat stress. So in summer it pays to be especially prompt in getting fish back into the water-- and avoid laying them on the sizzling hot deck when you take out the hooks. Find a shady or wet spot to work on them--the motor well, for example.

Wading fishermen usually have good luck with survival of released fish because the fish never have to be lifted completely out of the water. Just slip your fingers in behind the gill plate to steady them while you let the water support most of their body and work out the hooks. Reds treated this way rarely need much artificial respiration.

Handling Redfish

Don't get your fingers up inside the gills, though--hard on the fish, and hard on your fingers, too because they have sharp, bony plates in there that will catch and tear your skin. Grip the outer cover and you'll both come through it better.

Forget the lip-grip with reds. Though this grip quiets snook and largemouth bass, it doesn't impress a red. And holding up a heavy fish by the jaw is likely to damage his jaw, in any case. Also, it should go without saying-- but apparently doesn't--that you don't use the eye-socket grip with fish you want to release. This is a popular grip with commercial hook-and-line

Reds can be lifted by the gill plates, as former Tampa Bay Bucs footballer Scot Brantley shows here. But be careful not to slip your fingers inside the gill rakers. This can damage the gills, as well as your fingers.

grouper fishermen who are tossing everything directly into the ice box, and it does paralyze both grouper and reds--but it also blinds many. If you want to release a fish, leave its eyes alone.

Cold Weather Survival

In winter, reds seem pretty much bullet-proof. During freezing January nights, I've seen guys put reds in a bucket with no water, keep them there for a full 30 minutes, and then decide they don't want to keep the fish after all.

Dropped back into the water, the "dead" fish swam off as if nothing had happened!

The eye-socket grip controls reds, but also is likely to blind them. Never use this grip on fish that will be released.

Apparently they were so cold that their oxygen needs went to near zero, sort of suspended animation, and they were able to survive. This is not to recommend that you let reds lying around on deck if it's cold, but to indicate the durability of the species in the right conditions. Catch and release, obviously, is a lot more successful in winter.

Reds and Porpoises

A curious phenomenon is starting to take place in Florida and some other areas that may affect redfish survival to some degree. Porpoises, or bottle-nosed dolphins, are starting to figure out that fishing boats are putting back a lot of the fish they catch, and that those fish are easy targets.

There are some areas in Charlotte Harbor and Tampa Bay, both on Florida's west coast, where it's impossible to release a redfish--or a snook either--without having "Flipper" show up almost instantly and gulp down the free meal. A full-grown porpoise eats a 10-pound redfish like you'd gulp down a hotdog, after first coming up sideways with the fish in it's mouth to sort of show off its catch.

Porpoises are beautiful, intelligent animals with a natural right to the

105

bounty of the sea, but when they arrive on your fishing spot, the best thing you can do is pull up anchor and find another location if you have any hope of releasing fish undamaged.

Stretching The Limit

This might also be the spot to warn about size limits. Reds, like most other fish, will shrink slightly when killed and placed on ice for an hour or two. If you keep a redfish that measures exactly 18 inches long, that fish may be only 17 1/2 inches after some time on ice. If the Marine Patrol arrives to check your catch, he may find it's undersized, even though it was legal when it went in the box. Protect yourself by keeping only fish that give you a bit of leeway. (In more and more states, you can no longer avoid having your fish measured by filleting them immediately as you catch them. The fish have to be delivered to the docks in whole condition, and they'd best not be short if you want to avoid a fine.)

CHAPTER 13

ATLANTIC COAST REDS

REDFISH ON THE ATLANTIC COAST grow faster and live longer than those in the Gulf of Mexico, and the biggest of the big ones have historically been taken at the northern end of the range, in the surf of the Outer Banks of North Carolina and the islands of the Virginia coast.

Outer Banks Giants

In fact, 13 of the current 16 IGFA line-class records have come from this region, capped by David Deuel's monsterous 94-pound, 2-ounce all-tackle champ taken in November of 1984 at Avon, just north of Cape Hatteras. Every record fish over 50 pounds has come from this area. It has also turned out two of the five IGFA fly rod records, including the 42-pound, 5-ouncer caught by Floridian Chico Fernandez in May of 1981 on 12-pound tippet.

The Outer Banks region is a particularly hot fishery because it forms an "elbow" that juts far into the Atlantic. Cape Hatteras is almost 250 miles east of Jacksonville, Florida, to give you an idea. Thus, the land mass creates a giant eddy in the cold currents flowing along the coast from the north, and mixes them with the warmer water south of the Cape to create a great feeding ground where gamefish of all types abound. It doesn't hurt that massive Pamlico and Albemarle sounds dump their nutrient-rich waters here through Ocracoke, Hatteras and Oregon inlets, either.

Because of the northern location and the generally sub-tropical inclination of "spotted bass" as they're better known in the Carolinas, the fishery is good only from late March through November. During the colder months, the fish migrate, either going offshore to the warmth of the Gulf Stream or working south along the coast to Georgia and northern Florida.

Most of the big drum are caught in the surf, most on whole or cut blue crabs, menhaden or mullet, though the fish also readily hit 1- to 3-ounce chrome spoons, jigs and slow-sinking plugs. There are two peaks in the fishery, one from mid-March to mid-June, the other from early October to late November. Nine of the current line-class records were caught in November, most before the 15th.

There are a number of large piers on the Outer Banks, and all of these provide good spots to connect with a monster drum, even for those who can't make long throws with a big surf rod. Tackle must necessarily be heavy to control the giant fish around the pilings, however--50-pound-test gear is common.

Anglers with a four-wheel-drive vehicle can drive the beaches along most of the Outer Banks looking for leaping bait, hovering or diving birds or other signs of feeding areas. The trick for anglers new to the area is to survey the beach at low tide, looking for inshore holes deeper than the norm, as well as for breaks in the inshore bar that will become miniature passes as the tide surges through. As the water rises, these will become feeding areas. Most anglers like to fish the two hours on either side of high tide along the beaches.

Points with bars extending across the tide flow are also outstanding spots, though they draw lots of fishermen. These can be good when the water is going either way, so long as it's moving. Rough surf is no deterrent--the fish often bite best in troubled waters. (It can be very rough in November. Once a few years back I stayed there on the third story of a condo supported on pilings, and the wind gusts were literally creating waves in the water in the toilet!) And the big inlets--cuts through the long, thin arc of the barrier islands--are outstanding as falling tides pull tons of bait out of the backcountry. (You'll catch plenty of jumbo bluefish in these same areas as well as a now-and-then striped bass.)

If you can't figure out a good spot on your own, don't despair. Surf fishing is a major industry in the area, and there are plenty of guides who provide vehicle, tackle and an intimate knowledge of which sloughs produce when. See the "Guides" chapter for a listing, or you can book through most of the tackle stores in Buxton, which is sort of the surf fishing headquarters of the Outer Banks.

Pamlico Sound, the giant bay that backs the Outer Banks, also offers outstanding spring and fall "channel bass" fishing. Royal Shoal and Hodges Reef inside Ocracoke Inlet are good spots, as is Bryant Island Shoal. In fact,

David Deuel's monster 94-pound, 2-ounce drum taken near Avon, N.C. in November of 1984 stands as the all-tackle world-record. Most of the largest reds in the IGFA records have come from the Outer Banks of the Carolinas, most in November. (Photo courtesy Dare County Tourist Bureau)

Most of the Outer Banks beaches can be navigated with a four-wheel-drive beach buggy. Anglers search for active bait or diving birds to indicate feeding areas.

most points and bars in the sound hold fish at one time or another. So does the lower Neuse River, the mouth of the Pamlico River, and many of the other major flowages coming into the sound.

The remote beaches of Virginia's coastal islands also provide great spring and fall action, with some of the largest of all reds showing up here at times.

There's also good to outstanding summer fishing for smaller drum, to 10 pounds, in the inshore waters of most of the sounds and bays throughout the area. The same light tackle techniques that work elsewhere are effective here, including sight-casting when the schools are spotted in clear water.

Reds Of The Southern Shore

Though the Carolinas are truly the land of the giants, there are plenty of sizable reds further south along the Atlantic shore as well--and from the Georgia line southward, fishing is likely to be good all year around.

The many murky rivers that find their way to the sea along the Georgia coast load up with "rat" reds about 14 inches long in the fall as the young of the year reach legal size. At the same time, according to John Pafford, who heads the Coastal Recreational Fisheries program, mature reds to 30

The Atlantic beaches offer scenic beauty and monster reds, especially in fall during the spawn.

pounds show in the surf along the barrier islands, and in Altamaha Sound. Pafford says the mature fish are still abundant, but severe winters and excessive fishing pressure have been hard on younger fish the last five years. He's hopeful that a recently instituted 10-fish bag limit and a two-over-32" limitation on adults will bring the fishery back, if the weather helps.

Pafford also reported that ultrasonic tagging studies indicate the mature fish move offshore 8 to 20 miles in winter, and many of these return to the same stretch of beach each spring--there was no southward migration. He said that inshore juveniles rarely traveled more than 10 miles from where they were originally tagged.

Georgia reds don't reach the sizes of those in the Carolinas--a 44-pounder is the state record--but they do get old. Biologists there aged one fish at 40!

In winter, the inshore fish often move out on mud flats warmed by the sun on afternoon high tides in many of the coastal rivers. They're caught on shrimp, cut fish, crabs and small jigs bumped along bottom, with the jigs often sweetened with a bit of bait.

Cross the Florida line and the character of the inshore water changes, becoming more tannin-stained black rather than red-brown murk, but the reds like it just as well. There's a huge run that fills up the lower St. Johns River each fall and winter, with the fish stacking into areas up to 45 feet deep, particularly over rocky bottom. The St. Johns jetties have a good fall run, as

111

Big fish for a little angler--too big, in fact. Under current Florida law, only reds between 18 and 27 inches long can be kept.

well, and there are often lots of fish around the Mayport ship basin. Most of these are in the five to 10 pound range.

Atlantic Coast redfishing is prime from Daytona Beach southward to Sebastian Inlet, with some very large fish to be found on the clear flats much of the year. The shallow water makes these areas good for light-line record attempts, and two of the current IGFA line classes are held by fish from the

Indian River near Cocoa. Two fly rod tippet classes were also taken here, both in 1990, both by Dick Pope, Jr. Fish of 20 to 30 pounds are not uncommon, and some anglers have hooked fish they believe would approach 50 pounds.

Interestingly, under current Florida law, none of these lunkers can be kept because they all exceed the 18- to 27-inch slot limit established several years ago. Record anglers have taken to carrying certified scales on the water. When a lunker is landed, the angler steps overboard in the shallows with his scales--it's not acceptable per IGFA rules to weigh the fish inside a boat. The weight is recorded, the length measured, photos of fish, angler and tackle are taken, the catch is witnessed, and then the fish is released to fight again.

Prime areas include Mosquito Lagoon, particularly the spoil islands around the ICW channel as well as the southern tip of the big bay, which is closed to all commercial nets--and the Indian River from Titusville to Melbourne. The prime weapon here is the gold spoon, but lots of anglers also tangle with lunkers on flyrod streamers. Live finger mullet are also a favorite bait of patient fishermen who specialize in fish over 20 pounds. September and October are the best months for big fish, but spring is also productive.

There are redfish around Sebastian Inlet at times in the fall, and sometimes a lot of big ones as schools chase the annual mullet migration southward along the beaches. Live finger mullet fished around the jetties account for some whoppers, as well as for some huge snook and tarpon. Some reds are caught all the way down to Key Largo, the start of the Florida Keys, but the decreasing access to brackish water backcountry reduces the redfish populations here. Of course, there are loads of reds around the outflows of the rivers that come out of the Everglades, but we'll consider them in the next chapter, on Gulf Coast redfish.

113

CHAPTER 14

GULF COAST REDS

GULF COAST REDFISH don't quite attain the awesome sizes of their larger cousins on the Atlantic shore, but they make up for it by presenting themselves in considerable numbers, often in knee-deep water where they're susceptible to capture by flyrod as well as light spinning and baitcasting gear.

The Texas Coast

The redfish revival can rightly be said to have started on the Texas coast, where the early efforts of the Coastal Conservation Association grew out of the concerns of shallow-water redfish chasers tired of seeing their flats wiped out by excessive net harvest. Their efforts resulted in a net ban that was the first step in recovery of that fishery, as well as an historic first step in the inshore conservation movement among anglers nationwide.

The flats of the Laguna Madre, a clear, shallow basin behind the coastal barrier islands that stretch from the Mexican border to Corpus Christi, offer outstanding redfish action in a remote land surrounded for the most part by the million-acre Kenedy Ranch to the west and by Padre Island National Seashore to the east. It's big country where marina facilities are sometimes a hundred miles apart, and where the only human habitations are fishing cabins built on stilts along the waterway.

In some areas, there are dozens of these structures, most with their own diesel generators to power the cabin lights, as well as those that hang over the water to attract trout and reds after dark. During the week, few of the cabins are occupied and the only sounds after the generator shuts down are likely to be the splash of fish chasing mullet and the howl of coyotes across the ICW.

The "flats scooter" was invented here, and it's still the most popular of rigs for buzzing over water that's scarcely ankle deep. The scooters are table-top flat, sled-looking affairs with a tunnel down the middle to send water to a motor that's jacked far up off the normal transom position. The boats will skip across shallows that are about 6 inches deep, but many anglers use them primarily for transport, rather than fishing. In Texas, just about everybody wades when they get serious about catching redfish.

Gold spoons work fine for reds on these flats, but a lot of the regulars insist on catching their fish on topwaters like the Zara Spook, Jumpin' Minnow, Bomber Long A and the Redfin. These are a double-threat here, because they readily catch the jumbo trout that abound, thanks to Texas' "no-nets" rule for all inshore waters, as well as big reds.

Plastic-tailed jigs also catch lots of fish. Texans prefer long-tailed jigs such as the Kelly Wiggler, which has a shrimp-tail about four inches long. Some anglers put a stinger hook in the aft portion of these lures if they're fishing open bottom, though the tight Texas limits--three fish daily from 20 to 28 inches long at this writing--make it wise to avoid the extra hook any time fish are abundant. They usually are, once you begin to learn the flats; guides like Doug Bird out of Corpus Christi frequently catch and release 50 per day. Guides here usually include boat transport to one of the fishing cabins, food, lodging and tackle in their charter fees.

Bird suggests watching for structure in slightly deeper water as likely redfish concentration points. He notes that sometimes a single rock in a hole will be surrounded by reds. He also likes island points and the mouths of creeks on the tide flows, and the edge of the dredged ICW channel on low water. Fishing is best in spring and again in fall, as it is throughout much of the redfish range.

There are also plenty of reds in Aransas, Espiritu Santo, Matagorda, Trinity and Galveston Bays, though these fish are closer to the population centers of the Lone Star State and consequently see lots more lures buzzing overhead. Fishing methods are essentially the same in the shallows of all these areas as those described above for the Laguna Madre.

There's good fishing for "bull" reds of 20 to 30 pounds in the surf along the northern and central part of the coast, particularly in September and October. Anglers soaking live or cut bait off the fishing piers account for many of the big ones, which apparently move inshore from the large offshore schools to drop their eggs near the passes.

The reds caught most often on the Gulf Coast are not quite adults, though they're big enough to put up a great fight on light tackle. Female reds don't reach maturity until their fourth year, at a weight of 10 pounds or more.

This big female was caught on the Galveston Pier, in the years before the Texas slot limit was imposed. Fishing is still good along the beach of Galveston Island, but all the jumbos must be released.

The passes themselves are also good, with big, jettied entries like Sabine and Aransas loaded with jumbo redfish in the fall and early winter. Also good are smaller passes such as Rollover near Gilchrist, San Luis between Galveston and Freeport, and Cavallo near Port O'Connor. This latter pass can be reached only by boat, but it provides outstanding action at times.

Reds hang around well into winter most years, moving nearer deeper basins or ship channels where these are available. A few warm days in December may put plenty of fish back out on the flats--sometimes to their misfortune. Texas sometimes has major cold kills of redfish, trapped by "blue northers" that sweep in rapidly across the plains and stun the fish in the shallows.

To compensate for the kills and also for overfishing of years past, the state has the largest redfish stocking program in the nation, with millions of fry and fingerling put into the bays each year. Most coastal anglers say the

The jetty at South Pass, at the mouth of the Mississippi, is a gathering point for thousands of reds. The water is often rough and murky, but the fish don't seem to mind. Catches of 100 fish per day are not uncommon.

stocking is now having a very obvious impact on fishery numbers, and other states are researching similar stocking programs.

Louisiana/Mississippi/Alabama

The bayou and delta country shared by Louisiana, Mississippi and Alabama offers incredible redfishing, much of it so distant from population centers that many of the fish never see a hook.

Oil-rig fishing is one of the more unusual phenomena here. There are thousands of oil rigs throughout the area, some in water only a few feet deep, many more striding on offshore to water thousands of feet deep. All provide

119

good fishing, but only those inshore in water up to about 60 feet deep are redfish magnets. Reds hang around the pilings much of the time, but those active platforms with lots of electric lights and lighted gas flares really come to life after dark. On the "hot" rigs, endless trains of 15- to 20-pound reds circle the platforms for hours, taking any lure dropped in front of them--so many fish that the fishermen usually wear out long before the bite stops.

As if this is not enough, there are also great numbers of fish prowling the channels of the Mississippi River delta. The main passes, particularly South Pass, get absolutely stiff with reds in the 10- to 15-pound class around the outside jetties throughout the warmer months. The fish school tightly and face into the muddy current, gulping down whatever comes their way.

It's often rough fishing as Gulf waves stack up against the outbound current, and fast-moving oil-tankers add to the danger, but for those who brave the water, there's a red on every drop of a 1-ounce jig, particularly if the jig is sweetened with a bit of shrimp or Pro-Bait. Guides Dave Ballay and Ronnie Groinier, among others, run guide operations to reach these fish out of the oil town of Venice, about 70 miles south of New Orleans. (See Chapter 18 for phone numbers of these and other guides.)

The islands further into the Gulf escape the murk of the Mississippi, and offer broad, sandy beaches facing the Gulf, backed by clear grass flats on the inshore side.

The Chandeleurs, part of Breton Island National Wildlife Refuge, are particularly productive for both reds and lunker trout. The islands are about 70 miles east of New Orleans, 25 miles south of Gulfport, Mississippi and 50 miles southeast of Dauphin Island, Alabama. Anglers from all three states make regular trips here, and charter operations offer houseboats for extended stays.

Small reds of 4 to 7 pounds are found in potholes in the grass flats on the back side of the islands, while bigger ones prowl the beaches facing eastward. On the back side, topwater plugs and spoons are the best bet, for reds as well as the abundant seatrout, but in the surf, the best offering is live finger mullet, which can be netted in the sloughs throughout the warmer months. The mullet are freelined in the breakers, and usually wind up being inhaled by reds of 15 pounds or so, bigger in the fall.

The nearby islands off Mississippi and Alabama, including Cat, Ship, Horn, Petit Bois and Dauphin also turn out reds in the surf, particularly in October when the spawners move in. Again, live bait is the best offering.

The beaches of the Chandeleur Islands offer outstanding action in a remote area that can only be reached by boat or plane. Charter operations provide mother-ships for overnighting, and smaller skiffs for daily fishing trips

Just about every major bay in all three states is also prime redfish country, with the best fishing usually in the fall and on into December. The fish become hard to find in January and February, and then turn on again in the spring.

One of the best-known areas, where hundred-fish days are possible, is Calcasieu Lake, near Lake Charles, Louisiana. Here, big Terry Shaughnessy, former NFL linebacker, runs a guide operation that produces incredible success both on the "lake", actually a brackish water bay, and on adjoining Sabine National Wildlife Refuge. The waters are shallow and generally murky, but they're loaded with reds most of the year. Shaughnessy and the

Big Terry Shaughnessy runs an outstanding redfish operation at Lake Calcasieu, actually a brackish bay in southwestern Louisiana. Best action here is in October and November.

five guides who work with him catch them on jigs, Rat-l-Traps and topwaters, with best action around the abundant oyster bars in the area. Shaughnessy's operation also provides shoreside accommodations--and you can combine a duck hunt with your redfishing if you go in the fall season. Redfish action remains hot through April, after which most of the reds head for the Gulf until October begins the cycle again.

CHAPTER 15

REDFISH BOATS

A FEW YEARS AGO there was no such thing as a "redfish boat", per se. Today, thanks to the redfish boom, there are a dozen or more, all built to similar parameters. Redfish boats in general are small, 15 to 20 feet long, light weight, 700 to 1,000 pounds, and very shallow of foot--able to float in 7 to 10 inches of water with the outboard up, and to run in little more than 12 to 16 inches on plane.

In short, they are dead ringers for the bonefish boats that spawned them, even though a lot of the new fleet of flats boats are specifically designed for chasing reds in the shallows.

There are dozens of designs now available, and the only way to tell which one will suit you best is to go for a test ride in as many as possible, either with friends or with friendly dealers. Each boat has it's own distinctive feel--some concentrate on maximizing fishing room, others on maximum storage. Some have lots of freeboard to keep you dry, others have minimum freeboard to prevent the boat from kiting in the wind. Some builders prefer almost no vee in the bottom aft, so that the boat floats high, while others go for moderate or lots of vee to provide a smooth ride in rough water.

There aren't many absolutes, but in general most anglers are happy with boats that offer a moderate vee bottom, a pocket at the transom to feed water to the outboard even at maximum trim, plenty of bow flair to keep down spray, the smallest possible console, to maximize useful fishing space and prevent snags on the backcast, and dry storage in every inch of the boat that isn't needed for something else. Emphasize the "dry". Every compartment needs channeled lids to drain off rain water and spray, the deeper the channels the better.

Some hulls, like the Shoalwater and many of the Texas scooter-style

Redfish boats need to be shallow of foot and light enough for easy poling. Most anglers prefer hulls in the 16 to 20-foot range.

boats, feature tunnel hulls that allow the outboard to be mounted very high. These boats can run several inches shallower than conventional hulls, though they give up a little in efficiency and top speed. The Shoalwater, in lengths to 22 feet, can zip along in just 6 inches of water!

Light boats are better than heavy ones, other things being fairly equal. A 700-pound hull poles a lot easier than an 1100 pounder. A lot of anglers like to run smaller outboards these days, both to save money at purchase time and later, on fuel. Smaller motors are also lighter, allowing the boat to get out of the hole quicker and float higher. Ninety-horse motors weighing under 300 pounds are popular with flats aficionados.

Most redfish anglers want a trolling motor on the bow, so your choice will need some flat gunnel space up there to mount it.

Well-known builders at present include Action Craft, Hewes, Hoog, Lake & Bay, Maverick, Permit, Shoalwater and Silver King. Hydra-Sports is putting together a state-of-the-art machine, as is Ranger. A new aluminum flats rig from Fisher shows promise. And Aquasport, Hydra-Sports, Mako and Pro-Line, among others, make shallow-draft 17-foot center consoles that do a good job on the flats and double as bay boats thanks to higher freeboard than the all-out flats machines. These boats are heavier than the specialty boats, and require at least 115 horses for satisfactory performance.

Tunnel-hull boats allow operation in water that's scarcely ankle-deep. Note the trolling motor on the bow. The guide, Larry Mendez, has a foot-control for this unit that can be operated from the tower.

Of course, if you can't afford these high-dollar rigs, you can get along just fine with a broad-beamed 16-foot aluminum jon boat, which is far lighter than any of them, and scoots along fine on 50 horses. The flat bottom will pound you in rough water and there's no dry storage, but you can run shallow, run cheap in a jon.

Rigging It Right

Whatever boat you choose, you'll want a tower of some sort, probably a poling tower over the outboard aft, that puts you up high enough so that you can see fish at a considerable distance. Some of the larger flats boats like the Shoalwater can handle a center tower 6 feet tall, but for most flats boats that's overkill.

Most anglers also find that they want a trolling motor on their flats rig, even though they may pole the boat in extreme shallows. The troller provides silent electrical power to ease upwind, and makes it much easier to fish alone than if you attempt to pole and cast solo. A pair mounted on the stern, with controls on the poling tower, make it easy to control the boat from a good vantage point. Or, you might make use of a bow-mount with foot control, to keep your hands free for casting.

You'll want a steel prop on your outboard for durability, perhaps a four-blader to provide a hot hole shot, or maybe one of the new "Torque Shift" jobs that shifts down for the hole shot, up for top end. And if you really get shallow-water fever, you might opt for a hydraulic transom jack that lets you slide the motor up and down while still keeping the thrust parallel with the surface of the water, and maybe a low water pickup as well, to make sure that the motor doesn't overheat as you jack up your high-tech surfacing prop. Bob's Machine Shop of Ruskin, Florida, (813) 645-3966, is one of the nation's top suppliers of both.

Trim Tabs

Not too long ago, trim tabs were considered the sign of a poorly-designed hull. A boat wouldn't need them, went the thinking, if the bottom was right.

That was then. Now, everything from 50-foot sportfishermen to 16-foot bonefish skiffs sport tabs, and their skippers all sing the praises of variable trim.

Tabs are particularly useful to the shallow-draft boats used on the flats in pursuit of redfish, as well as snook and trout.

Trim tabs are flat pieces of metal mounted on the transom at the point where the bottom joins it, and are controlled by hydraulic or electrical means to move them up--to allow the stern to drop; or down--to raise the stern higher. They work much like the stabilizer on the tail of an airplane.

The most obvious use is in getting a boat on plane. With tabs of the proper size, any hull will practically leap out of the hole--the tabs completely counteract the "squat" of many deep vees when power is first applied. The tabs do away with those disquieting moments when the boat seems to be climbing a steep hill, the engine laboring, the bow thrust so high that forward visibility is impossible. More important for the shallow water fisherman, the upward thrust at the stern keeps it from dropping into the hole, and prevents the prop from plowing into bottom. This is one of the prime reasons that more and more flats fishermen are going to tabs--they're practically standard equipment on poling skiffs these days because they allow many boats to get on plane in little more than a foot of water. Tabs are also effective at raising the stern a few inches when the boat is on plane, thus allowing it

Small center-consoles like the Hydra-Sports 1750, with a pocket at the stern to feed water to the prop at maximum trim, make good combination boats for flats and bays. The minimal bow height allows use of an electric motor forward.

to run just a bit shallower than boats without tabs--and sometimes allowing you to cross miles of flats that others can't as a result.

Smoothing the Ride

Tabs are also useful in smoothing out rough water. Most boats have more vee at the bow than amidships and further aft, but on normal plane it's the back half of the bottom that takes the waves. With tabs, you can force the bow down, bringing that sharp vee into first contact with the seas. It splits them and noticeably eases the ride.

Alternatively, when spray or tall seas are coming over the bow, you may want to raise the front end of the boat to help your crew stay dry. By backing off on the tabs, you allow the stern to drop and the bow to rise--the effect is as if you have added several inches--or feet in the case of big boats--to your freeboard. You can do this to some extent with the trim on an outboard or sterndrive, but the tabs offer a more pronounced result--and are the only alternative with inboards.

What's more, you can raise just one side of the bow if you want. In open boats, this can be a tremendous help when you're running into seas from the bow quarter and the wind is giving you a cold shower with each wave. Though

Fully-planed off and with the motor trimmed high, a well-designed flats boat can skip across water only inches deep. Most have relatively flat bottoms to reduce draft.

every boat builder swears his hull is bone dry in this situation, in truth none are--the wind-blown spray is nearly inescapable. But with the tabs, you effectively cant the whole boat away from the spray, at the same time raising the windward side to help knock it down. The upwind tab is lowered slightly to cause that side of the boat to rise. The effect is remarkable--a 17-foot redfish boat can make a crossing nearly as dry as a 25-foot deep vee if the larger boat has no tabs to assist.

Tabs also help boats to remain on plane at lower speeds, since they add flat, planing surface aft. And most users report increases in speed--5 to 10 percent--and better fuel economy. The fuel economy really comes in when you're able to plane at lower speeds, running into rough seas. In fact, many tab converts say the units pay for themselves within a year thanks to the gasoline savings.

Tabs can also be used to correct imperfect designs, it's true. If your boat porpoises, plows or displays any other sins in running attitude, you can probably correct it with tabs. Remember, the same boat may behave in many different ways depending on the number of passengers aboard and where they're sitting, plus such other variables as the amount of fuel and ice aboard.

The Hewes line is considered one of the classics in flats boats. Note the minimal obstructions above the decks and the abundant storage hatches.

In a small boat, a heavy passenger on one side may cause a pronounced and uncomfortable lean. With tabs, you can drop the tab on that side and level out the boat, improving comfort, ride and safety.

Tabs come in standard or racing configurations. The standard models, best for most fishing boat applications, are wider than they are long, viewed from the transom. Racing models are longer, stronger and relatively narrow, best for boats that can exceed 50 miles an hour.

Don Kassing, an exec with Boat Leveler, Inc., recommends buying the largest tabs that will fit on your transom, so that the amount of control is maximized.

"Allow about 4 inches to the chine, 6 inches to the keel, and make sure it will clear the outdrive," says Kassing, who notes that most boat owners can handle their own installation of trim tabs. He says that large tabs create less drag overall because they don't have to be lowered so far to get the desired effect, thus help on top speed and fuel economy.

Prices range from $350 to around $700 for conventional tabs. Contact the following manufacturers for more information: Bennett Marine, (305) 427-1400; Boat Leveler, (314) 385-7470; Kiekhaefer Aeromarine, (414) 921-5330; Lenco/L. Saraga, (516) 349-7121; Teleflex Marine, (215) 495-7011.

CHAPTER 16

REDFISH COOKERY

A LOT OF ANGLERS are letting most of their redfish catches swim off to fight another day, but it does no harm to keep a few for the table now and then with the strict harvest rules now in place in most states throughout the range. The flesh of smaller reds--to 8 pounds or so--is light, moist, fine-grained and tasty in a wide variety of recipes. And reds are easily and quickly prepared.

Standard treatment is simply to slice a fillet off either side of the backbone, using a long, sharp knife. Reds have stout backbones, so there's no danger of slicing through and complicating the job if you keep the blade skimming along the vertebrae.

A good trick is to stop the cut aft just short of the tail, at the point where the meat runs out. You can then flip the filet over, slip the knife blade back in between the filet and the skin, and quickly strip off the skin, using the carcass as a "handle" as you lever the knife back and forth. It's a lot easier than trying to hold on to a slippery filet that has been cut free.

When the skin is off, you'll note a streak of soft, dark red meat down the center of each filet. This is the lateral line, and it tastes "fishy". If you don't like that taste--and most folks don't--remove the line by making a shallow cut on either side, angled toward the center, so that the line can be stripped away in a "V".

Finally, cut away the rib cage from the inside of the filet. This gives a boneless slab of meat that's ready for any recipe.

Storing

Reds, like most other fish, are best when cooked immediately. But they can be stored for weeks and even months if you water-pack them before freezing.

Simply make up portions of the size needed to feed your family, select appropriately-sized plastic freezer bags to fit these portions, and add the filets, cut into manageable chunks. Then partially fill the bags with water, enough to cover the filets completely. Zip the top of the bag shut except for a small opening at one end to allow excess air to escape, and "burp" the bag, pushing out all the air and sealing the top so that the entire filet is covered with the water. When this is placed in the freezer, the water seals in the juices, and the filet will never experience freezer burn, even if it's stored for months.

Recipes

One of the easiest and best ways to cook redfish is on the charcoal grill. A wire basket is required so that you can turn the filets without their falling apart, and so long as you're using the open fire, it's nice to add a few lumps of hickory or mesquite wood to add a tang of smoke to the flavoring.

Simply brushing the meat with mayonnaise is a good, basic recipe that usually draws raves. (You have to dry the filets to get the mayonnaise to stick.) The combination of shortening and eggs nicely browns the filets, and the touch of lemon juice is a nice spice. Leave the filets on the heat until they can be flaked with a fork, turning every five minutes.

The same system works well for redfish Teriyaki. Soak the filets for an hour in Teriyaki, then spray them lightly with a non-sticking agent such as Pam before placing them in the wire basket. Again, turn every five minutes until the filets begin to flake.

Redfish is wonderful when fried, especially via a waterside recipe favored by Sarasota, Florida, guide Pete Greenan, who does it regularly for his shore lunches. Pete uses peanut oil for frying, putting a couple inches in a skillet heated on his Coleman stove where it rests on the poling platform of his flats boat.

The redfish are filleted and skinned, cut in pieces about four inches square, and then dropped in a bag of Shake And Bake Seafood Flavoring. The filets are cooked until brown, drained on paper towels, then consumed in intemperate quantities with fried potatoes and onions.

Ashore, one of the better ways to cook reds is to bake them "in the shell", which is to say with the skin and scales still in place. This keeps the flesh remarkably moist, resulting in the tastiest of all redfish recipes, though you may want to disassemble the fish in the kitchen if you have guests sensitive to seeing creatures arrive at the table in whole condition. Remove the head, if you don't want your dinner looking back at you when you open

This red is just the right size for the table. The flesh will be firm, light and tasty in a variety of recipes.

the oven--but remember, each cut you make lets a bit of juice escape. The viscera, of course, are removed by splitting the ventral area from gills to anus.

Baking creates a sort of thick, sticky paste in the pan, so it's best to first line the pan with aluminum foil before placing the fish within. Some folks like to stuff the body cavity with orange quarters, apples or whatever, or you can put diced bacon in there to add flavor, and sprinkle some more on the top to trickle down and keep things moist.

Small reds are best filleted and fried. Larger fish are often baked whole "in the shell" with scales and skin left in place to hold in the moisture.

The fish should be baked about 90 minutes in a 350-degree oven, or until a fork easily penetrates all the way through the thickest part of the back area. Cooking time can vary considerably from oven to oven, so be sure to check every 15 minutes or so after the first hour.

CHAPTER 17

BIOLOGY, HABITAT AND MANAGEMENT

THE REDFISH LIFE-CYCLE is remarkably long, with some individuals living more than 60 years and attaining weights approaching 100 pounds. The journey from egg to fully-matured adult is a long one, taking the fish from the open sea to the tiniest mud creeks, across the inshore grass flats and estuaries, and finally back to the sea again. Thus, preservation of most types of natural coastal habitat are important to the life-cycle of the redfish.

Spawning

Reds spawn from August through mid-November in the Gulf of Mexico, with the peak in September and October. On the Atlantic Coast, spawning begins as early as July and may extend to December, but again the peak is September through October according to fisheries biologists. Spawning generally occurs at water temperatures warmer than 72 degrees F, and stops when water drops below 68 degrees F. The reduced hours of daylight also trigger the fall spawn, which occurs after days grow shorter than 10.5 hours. Scientists working with captive fish have been able to induce spawning by lowering water temperatures and shortening the hours of light supplied to the tanks. Male reds reach sexual maturity at ages 1 to 3, while females mature at ages 3 to 6.

Spawning occurs in the open Gulf and in the Atlantic in waters not far from shore, usually in depths less than 200 feet. Other major spawning areas are the passes and bay mouths that feed into these larger waters. In large bays, adult reds may spawn inside the embayment. Evidence of inshore spawning has been recorded in Florida's Tampa Bay and Mosquito Lagoon, among other locations.

The spawning activity is strongest on the new and full moons according to Florida Department of Natural Resources biologist Mike Murphy. The males chase the females for several hours, "drumming" loudly enough to be heard above the water at times. Spawning usually takes place just before dark, with milt and eggs released into open water. A female may release 2 million eggs per mating, and may spawn more than once a season.

Early Life

The fertilized eggs, about 1/25 inch in diameter, float with the tides for 20 to 30 hours before hatching into minute larval fish. The tiny wigglers spend another two to three weeks floating largely at the mercy of the sea, waiting for tidal currents to push them inshore. They feed on zooplankton, but if water temperature drops below 68 they stop feeding and many die.

The lucky ones that survive temperature changes and the massive predation during this time seek out survivable habitat--mud flats, grass flats, tidal creeks, oyster bars and mangroves, where they develop fins and begin to look like miniature redfish. Within a month, they're an inch long, and that rate of growth is likely to increase as the warmer temperatures of spring and summer arrive. By the end of the first year, the juveniles will be about a foot long.

Growth Rates

Atlantic Coast reds grow somewhat faster than Gulf Coast reds, and reach larger maximum sizes. The following chart shows the average length, in inches, of samples taken by biologists Mike Murphy and Ron Taylor of

REDFISH LENGTHS, ATLANTIC COAST											
Age	1	2	3	4	5	6	7	10	15	20	25
Length	15.1	24.0	29.9	33.7	36.2	37.9	39.0	40.5	41.0	41.0	41.1
REDFISH LENGTHS, GULF COAST											
Age	1	2	3	4	5	6	7	10	15	20	25
Length	13.4	22.9	28.9	32.6	35	36.5	37.5	38.7	39.0	39.1	39.1

the Florida DNR. Fewer specimens were taken in the larger sizes, thus not all ages are represented.

The largest fish sampled on the Atlantic Coast was 33 years old and 44.1 inches long. The largest sampled from the Gulf was 24 years old and 41.1 inches long. Note that reds grow rapidly until their fourth or fifth year, and then slow dramatically after that, sometimes gaining an inch per year, or less.

Interestingly, though Gulf reds grew slower, they put on more weight at a given length. Thus, a 35 1/2 inch Atlantic fish weighs around 12 pounds, 14 ounces, while a Gulf fish of similar length weighs around 13 pounds, 9 ounces.

Rat reds prefer to dine on shrimp and miniature crabs. As they increase in size, they eat more baitfish as well as larger crabs. The reliance on crabs, some environmentalists believe, make it critical that crab habitat--mangrove and mud flats--be maintained at optimal levels if redfish are to remain healthy.

In these days of catch-and-release fishing, it's interesting to know the weight of a fish of a given length. The following chart, prepared by Murphy and Taylor, gives approximate weights in pounds at various lengths. As you'll note from the chart, the difference between a 12-inch redfish, the size at which most used to be harvested, and an 18-incher is very considerable in terms of weight and usable meat. To get the best return per fish, it clearly pays to wait until at least the second year to harvest reds for food.

REDFISH WEIGHTS AT VARIOUS LENGTHS									
Inches	12	18	20	22	26	28	30	32	34	36
Weight	0.7	2.1	2.9	3.8	6.3	7.8	9.6	11.6	13.9	16.4

Redfish Migrations

The juvenile fish grow up in bays, brackish rivers and other estuarine areas, and are highly tolerant of low salinities, at times migrating into water that is completely fresh. The movement into coastal rivers is most common in winter when they seek warm-water springs to avoid cold snaps in the southern end of the range. Small reds can sometimes tolerate water as cold

It takes many years for a redfish to reach this size. The species has a life expectancy of more than 35 years.

Reds grow as much as an inch a month in their first year, and continue rapid growth until their fourth or fifth year. After that, they add only a few inches per year.

as 36 degrees, colder even than adults, but they prefer temperatures warmer than 60 degrees and will move to find warmer water. They don't move great distances, however. Tagging studies on the juveniles indicate that fish rarely move more than six miles from where they were spawned.

After reaching maturity, a considerable number of them migrate to offshore schools where they are thought to spend the rest of their lives except for occasional forays inshore during the fall spawn.

However, adults in some areas remain inshore permanently, feeding and spawning in larger bays and finding deep water refuge there in winter. (The adults must seek temperature refuge when water temperature drops below 50 degrees F, particularly if the drop is abrupt.) Adult fish are known to prefer high salinity waters, 20 to 40 parts per thousand, which may explain their offshore movement in many areas. It may also explain their presence in high-salinity bays like Florida's Mosquito Lagoon and the Indian River.

Atlantic Coast fish also migrate north and south with the seasons. The large offshore schools typically arrive in North Carolina waters from their wintering areas further south in March and April, and show up in Chesapeake Bay by May. They remain in these waters until October, and in the Carolinas until early November.

143

Most reds have only a single spot on their tails, but some are more liberally peppered. Note the minimal girth of this young fish. Reds put on weight rapidly after their first year, so limits that hold off harvest until at least the second year result in a greater yield per fish.

Adult Gulf Coast fish migrate somewhat with the approach of cold weather, leaving the bays and pushing offshore. There's also some westward movement of adult fish from the Alabama area toward the Breton Island areas off Louisiana in spring according to researcher R.M. Overstreet.

Redfish Management

Because reds spend so much of their juvenile lives within easy reach of commercial netters and inshore fishermen, fishing mortality can be very high if not controlled. In a Florida study in the late 1980's, biologists found that as little as .2 percent of young fish survived to sexual maturity in many estuaries. Since a 20 to 30 percent escapement to spawning age is necessary

The majority of reds caught by sportsfishermen today are being released. This has resulted in population increases in most states in the last two years.

to maintain most wild fish populations, regulations were obviously needed, and have been imposed in most states.

Florida currently has the tightest limits in the nation, with only one fish per day between 18 and 27 inches allowed. No harvest is allowed in March, April and May, and redfish may not be bought or sold.

Massive purse seine harvest in federal waters in the 1980's convinced fishery managers that the offshore spawners were too vulnerable to net capture, and that fishery, which took as high as a million pounds a month in the Gulf of Mexico, was shut down.

The current restrictive rules throughout the range appear to be working, with both redfish and redfishermen on the increase. So long as the habitat and water quality is protected, redfishing should remain excellent into the next millennium.

145

CHAPTER 18

GUIDES AND CHARTER OPERATIONS

REDFISH ARE OFTEN fairly cooperative once you find them, but knowing where to find them consistently is a full-time job. Thus the redfish guide can be a very important asset for both the vacationing angler visiting distant flats and the weekender who does not have enough time to stay on top of the fish movements. The guides are out there every day, year after year, and soon develop near-certain knowledge of when the schools will be where. If your angling time is limited, the guide can help you make the most of it, so that you can spend your day catching instead of looking--though even the best guides have those occasional bad days when they can't catch cold.

Rates for redfish guides vary by area of the country, from as low as $150 per day to as much as $350. This includes the guide's boat and gasoline. Sometimes it includes use of tackle, sometimes not--ask in advance. Ditto for live bait--some guides will castnet all the sardines you can use for free (though the time they spend at this is part of your angling day) and some will buy shrimp at the docks and add it to your tab. Again, ask before you book.

Most flats guides prefer to take only two clients per trip, though some will carry up to four. In some areas such as the Louisiana oil rig country, larger boats can be used, and larger parties can be carried. On the Outer Banks of the Carolinas, you can hire a surf-fishing guide, who will provide you with beach-buggy transport plus his knowledge of which sloughs produce on which tide phases--again, it's money well-spent for the out-of-town angler.

Here's a list of a few of the best, at this writing.

Dave Ballay, Venice, LA, (504) 534-9357
Doug Bird, Corpus Christi, TX (512) 937-3589

Phil Chapman, Lakeland, FL, (813) 646-9445
Corby Dolar, Homestead, FL, (305) 248-8712
Dennis Dube, Oldsmar, FL, (813) 855-9666
Dan Dyke, Buxton, NC, (919) 995-5083
Shawn Foster, Cocoa Beach, FL, (407) 784-2610
Pete Greenan, Charlotte Harbor, FL (813)923-6095
Ronnie Groinier, Venice, LA (504) 534-9357
Paul Hawkins, St. Petersburg, FL, (813) 894-7345
Richard Howard, Clearwater, FL, (813) 446-8962
Van Hubbard, Boca Grande, FL, (813) 697-6944
Kingfisher (Chandeleur Islands), Biloxi, MS, (601) 392-3448
Mike Locklear, Homosassa, FL, (904) 628-2602
Dave Markett, Tampa Bay FL, (813) 962-1435
Mac MacLawhorn, Ocracoke, NC, (919) 928-5921
Larry Mendez, Charlotte Harbor, FL, (813) 874-3474
Bill Miller, Charlotte Harbor, FL, (813) 935-3141
Norman Miller, Ocracoke, NC, (919) 928-5711
Frank Merillat, Buxton, NC (919) 995-5311
Chris Mitchell, Boca Grande, FL, (813) 964-2887
Scott Moore, Cortez, FL,(813) 778-3005
Phil O'Bannon, Fort Myers, FL, (813) 964-0359
Jim O'Neil, Bradenton, FL, (813) 794-5960
Dan Prickett, Chokoloskee, FL, (813) 695-4573
Dennis Royston, Hudson, FL, (813) 863-3204
Frank Schiraldi, Crystal River, FL, (904) 795-5229
Kenny Shannon, Venice, FL, (813) 497-4876
Terry Shaughnessy, Hackberry, LA, (318) 762-3391
Russ Sirmons, St. Petersburg, FL, (813) 526-2090
Southern Belle (Chandeleur Islands) Biloxi, MS (601) 436-6570
Tom Tamanini, Tampa Bay, FL, (813) 581-4942
Johnny Walker, Sarasota, FL, (813) 922-2287
Earl Waters, Homosassa, FL, (904) 628-0333
James Wood, Terra Ceia, FL, (813) 722-8746

Guides spend most of their time on the water and stay in touch with seasonal movements of fish year around. Their fee is money well spent for an angler learning the redfishing ropes.

FOR THE
INSHORE FISHERMEN
WHO ALSO FISH FOR
FRESH WATER BASS!
LARRY LARSEN'S BASS SERIES LIBRARY!

**1. FOLLOW THE FORAGE FOR BETTER BASS ANGLING -
VOLUME 1 BASS/PREY RELATIONSHIP** - The most important key
to catching bass is finding them in a feeding mood. Knowing the predominant forage, its activity and availability, as well as its location in a body of
water will enable an angler to catch more and larger bass. Whether you fish
artificial lures or live bait, you will benefit from this book.

SPECIAL FEATURES
- o PREDATOR/FORAGE INTERACTION
- o BASS FEEDING BEHAVIOR
- o UNDERSTANDING BASS FORAGE
- o BASS/PREY PREFERENCES
- o FORAGE ACTIVITY CHART

2. FOLLOW THE FORAGE FOR BETTER BASS ANGLING -
VOLUME 2 TECHNIQUES - Beginners and veterans alike will achieve more success utilizing proven concepts that are based on predator/forage interactions. Understanding the reasons behind lure or bait success will result in highly productive, bass-catching patterns.

SPECIAL FEATURES
- o **LURE SELECTION CRITERIA**
- o **EFFECTIVE PATTERN DEVELOPMENT**
- o **NEW BASS CATCHING TACTICS**
- o **FORAGING HABITAT**
- o **BAIT AND LURE METHODS**

3. BASS PRO STRATEGIES - Professional fishermen have opportunities to devote extended amounts of time to analyzing a body of water and planning a productive day on it. They know how changes in pH, water temperature, color and fluctuations affect bass fishing, and they know how to adapt to weather and topographical variations. This book reveals the methods that the country's most successful tournament anglers have employed to catch bass almost every time out. The reader's productivity should improve after spending a few hours with this compilation of techniques!

SPECIAL FEATURES
- o **MAPPING & WATER ELIMINATION**
- o **LOCATE DEEP & SHALLOW BASS**
- o **BOAT POSITION FACTORS**
- o **WATER CHEMISTRY INFLUENCES**
- o **WEATHER EFFECTS**
- o **TOPOGRAPHICAL TECHNIQUES**

4. BASS LURES - TRICKS & TECHNIQUES - Modifications of lures and development of new baits and techniques continue to keep the fare fresh, and that's important. Bass seem to become "accustomed" to the same artificials and presentations seen over and over again. As a result, they become harder to catch. It's the new approach that again sparks the interest of some largemouth. To that end, this book explores some of the latest ideas for modifying, rigging and using them. The lure modifications, tricks and techniques presented within these covers will work anywhere in the country.

SPECIAL FEATURES
- o **UNIQUE LURE MODIFICATIONS**
- o **IN-DEPTH VARIABLE REASONING**
- o **PRODUCTIVE PRESENTATIONS**
- o **EFFECTIVE NEW RIGGINGS**
- o **TECHNOLOGICAL ADVANCES**

5. SHALLOW WATER BASS - Catching shallow water largemouth is not particularly difficult. Catching lots of them usually is. Even more challenging is catching lunker-size bass in seasons other than during the spring spawn. Anglers applying the information within the covers of this book on marshes, estuaries, reservoirs, lakes, creeks or small ponds should triple their results. The book details productive new tactics to apply to thin-water angling. Numerous photographs and figures easily define the optimal locations and proven methods to catch bass.

SPECIAL FEATURES
- o UNDERSTANDING BASS/COVER INTERFACE
- o LOCATING BASS CONCENTRATIONS
- o ANALYSIS OF WATER TYPES
- o TACTICS FOR SPECIFIC HABITATS
- o LARSEN'S "FLORA FACTOR"

6. BASS FISHING FACTS - This angler's guide to the lifestyles and behavior of the black bass is a reference source of sorts, never before compiled. The book explores the behavior of bass during pre- and post-spawn as well as during bedding season. It examines how bass utilize their senses to feed and how they respond to environmental factors. The book details how fishermen can be more productive by applying such knowledge to their bass angling. The information within the covers of this book includes those bass species, known as "other" bass, such as redeye, Suwannee, spotted, etc.

SPECIAL FEATURES
- o BASS FORAGING MOTIVATORS
- o DETAILED SPRING MOVEMENTS
- o A LOOK AT BASS SENSES
- o GENETIC INTRODUCTION/STUDIES
- o MINOR BASS SPECIES & HABITATS

7. TROPHY BASS - is focused at today's dedicated lunker hunters who find more enjoyment in wrestling with one or two monster largemouth than with a "panfull" of yearlings. To help the reader better understand how to catch big bass, a majority of this book explores productive techniques for trophies. The "how to" information was gleaned from professional guides and other experienced trophy bass hunters. This book takes a look at the geographical areas and waters that offer better opportunities to catch giant bass.

SPECIAL FEATURES
- o GEOGRAPHIC DISTRIBUTIONS
- o STATE RECORD INFORMATION
- o GENETIC GIANTS
- o TECHNIQUES FOR TROPHIES
- o LOCATION CONSIDERATIONS
- o LURE AND BAIT TIMING

8. AN ANGLER'S GUIDE TO BASS PATTERNS examines the most effective combination of lure, method and places. Being able to develop a pattern of successful methods and lures for specific habitats and environmental conditions is the key to catching several bass on each fishing trip. Understanding bass movements and activities and the most appropriate and effective techniques to employ will add many pounds of enjoyment to the sport of bass fishing. "Bass Patterns" is a reference source for all anglers, regardless of where they live or their skill level.

SPECIAL FEATURES
- o BOAT POSITIONING
- o NEW WATER STRATEGIES
- o DEPTH AND COVER CONCEPTS
- o MOVING WATER TACTICS
- o WEATHER/ACTIVITY FACTORS
- o TRANSITIONAL TECHNIQUES

9. BASS GUIDE TIPS focuses on the most productive methods of the top bass fishing guides in the country. This book is loaded with sometimes regionally-known techniques that will work in waters all around the country. Often such "local knowledge" remains regional or lake-specific, but this book explains how one productive tactic on a southern lake might be just as productive on waters in the midwest or north.

SPECIAL FEATURES
- o SHINERS, SUNFISH KITES & FLIES
- o FLIPPIN', PITCHIN' & DEAD STICKIN'
- o BRACKISH WATERS & BASS SIGNS
- o FRONTS, HIGH WINDS & RAIN
- o MOVING, DEEP, HOT & COLD WATERS

CPSIA information can be obtained
at www.ICGtesting.com
Printed in the USA
BVOW11s0315080717

488838BV00004B/4/P